MW00620613

ENCYCLOPEDIA OF BRITISH, PROVINCIAL, AND GERMAN ARMY UNITS 1775-1783

ENCYCLOPEDIA OF BRITISH, PROVINCIAL, AND GERMAN ARMY UNITS 1775-1783

Philip R. N. Katcher

Stackpole Books

ENCYCLOPEDIA OF BRITISH, PROVINCIAL
AND GERMAN ARMY UNITS—1775-1783

Copyright©1973 by
THE STACKPOLE COMPANY

Published by
STACKPOLE BOOKS
Cameron and Kelker Streets
Harrisburg, Pennsylvania 17105

Printed in the U.S.A.

Library of Congress Cataloging in Publication Data

Katcher, Philip R   N
   Encyclopedia of British, provincial, and German
army units, 1775-1783.

   Bibliography: p.
   1. United States--History--Revolution--British
forces. I. Title.
E267.K37   973.3'41   72-11881
ISBN 0-8117-0542-0

to my parents

Contents

Introduction

STUDENTS OF THE War of American Independence sometimes overlook the fact that while Great Britain was fighting the war on North American shores she was simultaneously fighting on every continent of the world in the defense of her Empire.

In November, 1778, for example, the British Army had 16 cavalry and 23 infantry regiments in England, one cavalry and three infantry regiments in Scotland, 11 cavalry and 11 infantry regiments in Ireland, two cavalry and 45 infantry regiments in North America, seven infantry regiments in the Mediterranian, six infantry regiments in the West Indies, while one more was stationed in India and another in Africa. [1] Much of India, too, had to be defended by the Honourable East India Company's army of native troops and two European units—the Madras European Infantry Regiment and the East India Company's Bengal Regiment.

In the end, however, against the armies of France, Holland, Spain, Portugal, the Continental Congress and a host of lesser enemies, the British Army had managed not only to survive, but even to prevail. The 13 colonies in North America and Minorca were lost, but Gibraltar was saved and the Empire in the West Indies and India was enlarged. It was largely the men in the regiments in this book which made this possible.

For any book of this kind, one man alone can't possibly collect all the desired information without the help of many people. Many thanks, then, go to all those who helped out and especially in the United States, to Richard Claydon, Roy Vandegrift, Gustav Person, Vincent Kehoe, Thomas Dunbar, and Philip Cavanaugh of the U.S. Army Military

Research Collection. Elsewhere in the world, thanks is owed to G.A. Embleton of England; Major H. Barker, Regimental Museum of the Seaforth Highlanders; Major D. Baxter, The Northamptonshire Regiment Comrade's Association; William Boag, Scottish United Services Museum; Rene Chartbrand, National Historic Sites Services of Canada; Kenneth J. Collins, Maidstone Museums and Art Gallery; Lieutenant Colonel J.E.E. Fry, Regimental Museum of the Duke of Cornwall's Light Infantry; Colonel N.S. Pope, The Light Infantry Office (Yorkshire); E.J. Priestley, City of Liverpool Museums; Lieutenant Colonel J.D. Ricketts, The Worcestershire and Sherwood Foresters Museum; Major F.J. Reed, The Queen's Regiment; Peter R. Russell-Jones, The City of Manchester Art Galleries; Lieutenant Colonel M. Ryan, The Royal Warwickshire Regimental Museum; Lieutenant Colonel C.L. Speers, The Duke of Edinburgh's Royal Regiment; Major Stead, The Royal Anglian Regiment; Lieutenant Colonel A.W. Stansfield, The York and Lancashire Regiment; Lieutenant Colonel A.C.M. Urwick, The Light Infantry Office (Somerset), and Major A.J. Wallace, The Queen's Lancashire Regiment. I should also like to thank the staffs of the Royal Hampshire Regiment, the Gloucestershire Regiment, and the Museum and Public Library of Canterbury for their helpfulness.

Especially, I should also like to thank my wife for her helpfulness and many constructive ideas on this project.

Special thanks is due to artists Peter Copeland, Rebecca Katcher, Dennis Martin, Eric Manders, Don Troiani, Frederick Ray and George C. Woodbridge, of the Company of Military Historians and the Brigade of the American Revolution for so generously allowing me to use their excellent drawings.

While all of the foregoing contributed greatly, any errors, of course, are my responsibility.

P.R.N.K.

How to Use
This Book

EVERY MAJOR UNIT which served King George III between the years 1775 and 1784 is briefly covered in this book, although the emphasis is on those which served in the North American Theatre of Operations.

Basically, the book is organized into three sections: British regiments, Provincial units and German units. This has been done because the organization of the units and their way of designating themselves differ among the three types. In each case the listings contain, as much as available, the unit designation, a brief outline of its activities during the period, uniform notes and the commanders' names.

In the British section the units are listed as they were during the Revolutionary War; that is, the first two regiments of horse which served in America first, then the Royal Artillery Regiment, the three Guards Regiments, and the regiments of foot by numerical designation. The Marines, who did not receive their Royal designation until 1803, were then brigaded between the 49th and 50th Regiments of Foot, and their listing falls there. Officers are listed as in command "to war's end." However, a good number of the regiments remained organized and active in Royal service beyond the War, hence many of these officers continued in command for many more years.

Units in the Provincial section are listed alphabetically by their most common names. This may mean the commander's name, such as Emmerich's Chasseurs, or their official name, such as the South Carolina Royalists, or simply the name they commonly used, such as the

Queen's Rangers instead of the official 1st American Regiment. Other names are listed for cross-referencing.

The German section, too, is listed alphabetically. It was the general practice to designate the regiment after its chief, although in some cases this was not so. When the chief was changed, the regimental designation was also changed. In all cases the full regimental listing falls under the first designation the unit bore when it arrived in America. Later designations are listed and cross-referenced. As with the British regiments, the war's end did not mean the end of command, despite the fact that the commanders are often listed as commanding from some date, "to war's end."

An introduction to each section gives basic information on the structure of units, uniform, accoutrement and weapons.

The Army of
Great Britain

THE BRITISH REGULAR Army was made up of regiments of foot and horse, three regiments of foot guards and two of horse guards, the Royal Artillery Regiment and various staff officers. The Royal Engineers had its beginnings in 1772 as the Military Company of Artificers at Gibraltar. The Marines, who normally served aboard ship and fell under Royal Naval rule, could be used as infantry and were brigaded between the 49th and 50th Regiments of foot at those times.

The regiments of foot made up the "backbone" of the Army. There were 70 of those prior to the outbreak of hostilities and the Army was then enlarged, both by adding battalions to existing regiments and by forming new regiments. By the war's end, the Army had 105 Regular regiments of foot on its rolls. In addition, for guarding Great Britain itself, the government raised three Scottish Fencible Infantry regiments which could not serve away from the British Isles, in April, 1778. A fourth was added in February, 1779.

Each regiment was made up of eight battalion companies, one grenadier company and one light company initially, although other companies were later authorized. A regiment of 12 companies should have been made up of a colonel, a lieutenant colonel, a major, nine captains, 14 lieutenants, 10 ensigns, one chaplain, an adjutant, a quartermaster, a surgeon and his mate, 36 sergeants, 36 corporals, 24 drummers, two fifers and 672 privates, for a total of 811 men. The privates included three "contingent" men per company. These men were simply names added to the muster-rolls and the money paid to these nonexistent men would be used as the colonel or company commander wanted—fancier uniforms, funds for widows and families, or whatever. In actual field practice, each company had about 25 effective men.

The grenadier company was made up of the tallest and strongest men in the regiment. Originally, they had been used to throw grenades into fortifications on the attack, but by now the grenade was no longer used and the only leftovers of their past function were the brass cases in which they used to carry lit matches, worn on their cartridge box slings. The grenadiers were considered the "elite" of the regiment, and wore short swords and tall bearskin caps with fancy metal plates in front instead of the cocked hats of the battalion men. The company was stationed on the right of the regiment when it was drawn together on line.

The other flank company was the light company. This company was to be made up of quite physically-fit men and was used in a ranger or scouting manner, usually. The men had their coats cut short and wore leather caps, red waistcoats, small cartridge boxes and carried hatchets.

The two flank companies throughout the war generally were brigaded with other such companies and rarely served with their battalion companies. As listed herein and unless otherwise specifically stated, the regimental movements refer to the battalion without its flank companies.

If the battalion was the "heart" of the regiment, the private soldier was the "heart" of the battalion. He was armed with the 15-pound, .75 caliber flintlock "Brown Bess" and its foot-long bayonet. He wore plain black shoes usually buckled with slightly rounded brass buckles, over which he wore heavy linen half or full gaiters. His breeches and waistcoat were of white linen or wool, although in the winter long wool trousers were commonly issued instead of breeches. Highland regiments wore kilts of the government sett, the modern Black Watch tartan, although many of them wore heavy linen trousers during various campaigns.

Early in the war, he had worn his bayonet in a belt around his waist, but

A typical brass engraved waistbelt worn by officers. (Drawing by Rebecca Katcher)

A sergeant of grenadiers. The brass case on the cartridge belt sling was designed to hold a lit match which was used to light grenades. At this time it was strictly a mark of the grenadier. (Drawing by George C. Woodbridge, courtesy of the *Brigade Dispatch*.)

later it became the custom to sling the waistbelt around his body from his right shoulder. His coat was of brick red wool, reaching almost to the pan of his knee, lined either wholly or partly in white wool. It had a flat collar, long lapels and a round cuff of a different, or facing, color which distinguished his regiment. His regiment was also distinguished by the number

A cuff of a reproduction regimental coat of the 42nd Regiment of Foot showing regimental lace. The lace was of white worsted wool with stripes of different colors according to the regiment. It was placed around each buttonhole in bastion loops, as shown, or in rectangles.

on his pewter buttons and by the white wool tape, called lace, sewn around his buttonholes. This was usually sewn in rectangular shape, although some regiments used five pointed, or "bastion" shape lace. Woven into the lace were different colors. His coat's two outside pockets were false while his one real pocket was sewn into the inside skirts of his coat.

Across his other shoulder he wore his cartridge box of black leather, suspended by a whitened buff leather sling. The box contained anywhere from only 18 up to 30 rounds of ammunition. The box's flap was decorated in many cases by a brass plate, often with a regimental number in a circle under a crown.

British cartridge box badge. Used both by Regular and Provincial troops, at least one example has been found with a regimental designation engraved in the brass circle around the GR cypher.

The Army of Great Britain

On the march he carried his haversack. This was a large envelope of linen—shut with three plain pewter buttons and slung across his right shoulder. In it was his food; on top of it was a tin canteen.

Early in the war the average knapsack was worn over the shoulder, generally on the left side, while the haversack was worn on the right. Later, the more modern "square-on-the-back" pattern of knapsack became more popular. Many of the later knapsacks were of painted canvas, although most were of brown or white goatskin.

This knapsack is probably typical of canvas knapsacks adopted by British and Provincial units late in the war. (Courtesy of the National Army Museum.)

The same basic uniform was worn by a private in the mounted regiments serving in America. In place of the cocked hat, however, was worn a helmet of metal or hard leather. From the right shoulder hung a straight light dragoon's sabre and from the other hung a wide belt on which was hooked a carbine—a short "Brown Bess."

The Guards regiments, which contributed 15 men from each of their companies for a composite Guards battalion in America, were uniformed largely the same as the regular "marching" battalions, although there were many minor differences in their uniforms.

Sergeants wore scarlet instead of brick red, wool coats and plain white lace around their buttonholes. Their hats, and sometimes even their buttonholes, were bound up in silver, and they wore a sash of scarlet worsted with a stripe of the regimental facing color in the sash's center. They also carried short swords, or "hangers." The only marking for a corporal was a silk epaulette or an aiguillette of white or yellow, depending on the officers' metallic colors, worn on the right shoulder.

The officer's coat was much the same as the sergeant's. Each regiment was assigned silver or gold metallic colors for the officers to wear and therefore their buttons were either of silver or other gilt metal. In addition, many officers either embroidered their buttonholes or had metallic lace sewn around their buttonholes. Hats were often bound up with metallic lace, too.

At the war's beginning, officers commonly wore their swords hanging from waistbelts worn under their waistcoats. A crimson net silk sash was worn around the waist and knotted on the left for officers of foot, and on the right for officers of horse. As the period progressed, however, it became the custom to wear the sword suspended in a whitened buff leather belt from over the right shoulder. Usually an oval belt plate, often engraved with a regimental marking, was worn in the center of the belt. A scarlet and gold sword knot was worn around the sword grip and the grip, itself, was gold or silver depending again on the regimental metal.

On duty the officer usually wore a rounded metal half-moon-shaped gorget around his neck. This was tied with a piece of ribbon of the facing color and usually engraved with the Royal Coat of Arms or a regimental badge.

Officers of horse were armed with their sabers, like the other ranks, but theirs were better made. They usually had a brace of flintlock pistols in their saddles. The men had pistols in their saddles, too, but ones of poorer quality.

Officers of foot usually carried spontoons. These were long poles with an iron spearhead at the end. Grenadier officers and officers in some regiments wore cartridge boxes and carried fusils, or lighter and better-quality muskets.

All the regimental officers in a regiment of foot wore a single epaulette on the right shoulder, while officers in regiments of horse wore a single epaulette on the left one. Men were simply expected to recognize their officers by their features. Colonels wore two epaulettes. The rank of colonel, however, was generally given to someone who would not actually command in the field. For example, the colonel of the 43rd Regiment of Foot was Major General Sir William Howe, K.B., who commanded the entire British Army in the 13 rebelling colonies, although the 43rd was but one

A reconstruction of typical British battalion officer's dress in the field. The officer's hat is gold laced. His coat is embroidered in gold and his buttons are gold. All battalion officers wore a single epaulette on their right shoulders. His sword is carried on a waistbelt worn under his waistcoat, and he has a crimson silk net sash knotted on the left side. He carries a spontoon. (Photo of Arthur Blundell, courtesy of *Soldier* Magazine.)

regiment. Also, Lieutenant General John Burgoyne commanded the 16th Regiment of Light Dragoons which was serving in New York and Philadelphia while the general was away meeting disaster at Saratoga.

In such a case, command of the regiment fell actually on the lieutenant colonel, but at times he, too, might be away filling some higher post and the actual commander might be the regiment's major.

As herein listed, both the colonels' and lieutenant colonels' names are given along with the commander, if there was a man holding the rank of colonel who commanded under the official regimental colonel.

In August, 1782, each foot regiment in the British Army which had been previously known simply by number or an "ancient" name, was assigned a shire designation. These are also given. In the listings the ancient regimental title is also given in parenthesis along with the numerical designation. Many of these British regiments still exist today, although the passage of time has caused many amalgamations, changes and reductions in units and their designations. Where available, the exact way the original regiment is referred to as of August, 1972, is given in the listings. These often reflect the old designations, as for example the 16th/5th Queen's Royal Lancers once made up of the old 16th Light Dragoons and the 5th Dragoons. Most infantry regiments, however, are quite different today.

BRITISH HORSE REGIMENTS

16th (Queen's Own) Regiment of Light Dragoons   Formed as the 16th Light Dragoons, 1759, and designated the 2nd Queen's Light Dragoons, 1766. Renumbered the 16th, 1769. Arrived at New York September, 1776. Sent on the 1777 Philadelphia campaign, fighting at Brandywine and Paoli. Returned with the Army to New York, 1778, fighting at Monmouth Court House. As an understrength regiment, men transferred to the 17th Regiment of Light Dragoons, and officers returned to the British Isles, where the regiment spent the rest of the war, December, 1778. Uniform: Blue facings, yellow lace with one blue stripe; officers' metal, silver. Today: 16th/5th Queen's Royal Lancers.[2]

    COLONEL: Lieutenant General John Burgoyne, to 1780

            Major General Hon. William Harcourt, 1780 to war's end

    COMMANDER: Colonel Hon. William Harcourt, 1777-1780

            Colonel Sir Robert Laurie, Bt., 1782 to war's end

    LIEUTENANT COLONEL: Hon. William Harcourt, to 1777

            Sir Robert Laurie, Bt., 1777-1782

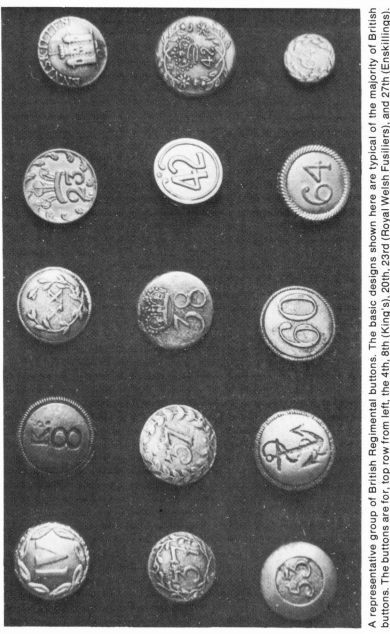

A representative group of British Regimental buttons. The basic designs shown here are typical of the majority of British buttons. The buttons are for, top row from left, the 4th, 8th (King's), 20th, 23rd (Royal Welsh Fusiliers), and 27th (Enskillings). Second row, from left, two types used by the 37th, the 38th, and two types used by the 42nd (Royal Highland). Third row, 53rd, Marines, 60th (Royal American), and two types used by the 64th Regiment of Foot. Two or three different designs were commonly used within the same regiment at the same time.

The 16th (Queen's) Regiment of Light Dragoons. The figures are, from left, a sergeant, farrier, trumpeter, officer and corporal. (Drawing by Peter Copeland, courtesy of The Company of Military Historians.)

17th Regiment of Light Dragoons Formed as the 18th Light Dragoons, 1759, and renumbered 17th, 1763. Designated 3rd Light Dragoons, 1766, being returned to 17th designation, 1769. Arrived at Boston May, 1775. Sent on 1776 New York campaign, fighting at Long Island, Fort Washington and Princeton. Elements in New York served at Forts Clinton and Montgomery, 1777. The rest sent on 1777 Philadelphia campaign, fighting at Whitemarsh. Returned with the Army to New York, 1778, fighting at Monmouth Court House. Fought at Pound Ridge, N.Y., skirmish. One troop served with the British Legion in the southern campaigns, fighting at Cowpens, Guilford Court House and interned at Yorktown. Regiment returned to England, 1783. Uniform: White facings, white lace with a black edge, brass helmets; officers' metal, silver. Today: 17th/21st Lancers.

COLONEL: Major General George Preston, to 1782

Lieutenant General Hon. Thomas Gage, 1782 to war's end

COMMANDER: Colonel Samuel Birch, 1780 to war's end

LIEUTENANT COLONEL: Samuel Birch, to 1780

Oliver Delancy, 1781 to war's end (also served as adjutant general in America)

ARTILLERY

Royal Artillery Regiment Raised as The Train of Artillery and designated The Royal Artillery Regiment, 1716. In battalion, detachment and company units, served at virtually every post and battle of the war, with the 4th Battalion largely serving in America. Uniform: Blue coats faced red with plain yellow lace and plain brass buttons, yellow bindings on hats; officers' metal, gold. Today: The Royal Artillery Regiment.

COMMANDER IN AMERICA: General James Pattison[3]

GUARDS REGIMENTS

1st Regiment of Foot Guards Formed as The King's Royal Regiment of Guards, 1660, and designated 1st Regiment of Foot Guards, 1685. From each company 15 men picked and posted to a composite Guards Regiment which served in America, while the rest of the regiment remained in the British Isles. Arrived at New York July, 1776, fighting at Long Island and Fort Washington. Sent on the

A gunner of the 4th Battalion, the Royal Artillery Regiment. Note the cannon instruments on the cartridge box sling. The plume on the hat was a special marking of the 4th Battalion. (Drawing by Don Troiani, courtesy of the *Brigade Dispatch*.)

Coldstream Guards

1777 Philadelphia campaign, fighting at Brandywine. Returned with the Army to New York, 1778, fighting at Monmouth Court House. Fought at Springfield, N.J., 1777. Sent to Charleston August, 1781, fighting at Cowan's Ford, N.C.; Guilford Court House; Green Spring, Va., and interned at Yorktown. Uniform: Blue facings, plain white lace; officers' metal, gold. Today: The Grenadier Guards.

COLONEL: Lieutenant General The Duke of Gloucester

Coldstream Guards Formed as Colonel Monck's Regiment of Foot, 1650, and designated The Lord General's Regiment of Foot, 1661. Made foot guards, 1661. Designated The Coldstream Regiment of Foot Guards, 1670. History and uniform in America same as 1st Regiment of Foot Guards (which see.) Today: The Coldstream Guards.

COLONEL: General John Earl of Waldegrave

3rd (Scots) Regiment of Foot Guards Formed 1660 as The Scots Regiment of Guards and designated 3rd Regiment of Foot Guards, 1713. History and uniforms in America same as the 1st Regiment of Foot Guards (which see.) Today: The Scots Guards.

COLONEL: General John Earl of Loundon, to 1782
General John Duke of Argyll, 1782 to war's end

BRITISH FOOT REGIMENTS

1st (Royal Scots) Regiment of Foot (The Royal Regiment) Formed 1633 as Hepburn's Regiment of Foot, then designated Le Regiment De Douglas, 1637, and the Earl of Dunbarton's Regiment, 1653. Designated The Royal Regiment of Foot, 1688, and then 1st Regiment of Foot, 1751. Stationed in the British Isles, with the 1st Battalion being sent to Barbadoes January, 1781, then to St. Kitts, where captured, January, 1782. Uniform: Blue facings, lace with one blue worm; officers' metal, gold. Today: The Royal Scots (The Royal Regiment).

COLONEL: General John Duke of Argyll, to 1783
Lieutenant General Lord Adam Gordon, 1783 to war's end
LIEUTENANT COLONEL: Rudolph Bentinck, to 1777
William Dundas, 1776-1778

A musicians coat of the 1st Regiment of Foot Guards. The lace used is Royal lace and the buttons are plain pewter. (Courtesy of the National Army Museum.)

2nd Regiment of Foot

> Thomas Fraser, 1777-1781
> James Lumsdaine, 1778 to war's end
> Frederick Thomas, 1779-1783
> Archibald Campbell, 1783 to war's end

2nd (Queen's Own) Regiment of Foot   Formed as The Tangier or Queen's Own Regiment of Foot, 1661, and designated The Queen Dowager's Regiment of Foot, 1685. Then The Queen's Royal Regiment of Foot, 1703; The Princess of Wale's Own Regiment of Foot, 1715; The Queen's Own Regiment of Foot, 1727, and the 2nd (Queen's Own), 1751. Sent from Gibraltar to England, January, 1775. Helped suppress the Gordon Riots, June, 1780. Returned to Gibraltar, November, 1783, after service as marines on the home fleet, June, 1782. Uniform: Blue facings, lace with one blue stripe; officers' metal, silver. Today: 1st Battalion/The Queen's Regiment.

> COLONEL: Lieutenant General Sir Charles Montague, K.B., to 1778
> Lieutenant General Daniel Jones, 1778 to war's end
> COMMANDER: Colonel William Hamilton, 1782 to war's end
> Colonel William Dalrymple, 1782 to war's end
> LIEUTENANT COLONEL: James Barker, 1776-1779
> William Hamilton, 1777-1782
> Michael Nickson, 1777-1779
> William Dalrymple, 1778-1782
> Thomas Wollocombe, 1783 to war's end

3rd Regiment of Foot (The Buffs)   Formed as a Holland Regiment, 1572, and became Prince George of Denmark's Regiment, 1659. First called The Buffs, 1747, and became 3rd Regiment of Foot, 1751. Shire assigned: East Kent. Sent from England to Ireland, 1775, and from Cork to Charleston, S.C., March, 1781, arriving there in June. Sent to the relief of Ninety Six, and fought at Eutaw Springs. Left Charleston for Jamaica, December, 1782. Uniform: buff facings, lace with red, black and yellow stripes worn in pairs officers' metal, silver.[4] Today: 1st Battalion/The Queen's Regiment.

> COLONEL: Lieutenant General Sir Jeffery Amherst, K.B., to 1779
> Major General William Style, 1779 to war's end
> COMMANDER: Colonel Alexander Stewart, 1782 to war's end
> LIEUTENANT COLONEL: John Biddulph, to 1779

Alexander Stewart, 1779-1782
Thomas Dawson, 1782 to war's end
James Abercromby, 1783 to war's end
William Madox Richardson, 1783 to war's end

4th (King's Own) Regiment of Foot   Formed as the 2nd Tangier Regiment, 1680, and designated the Duchess of York and Albany's Regiment of Foot, 1684, becoming the Queen's Own Regiment of Foot the following year. Made marines, 1702, and returned to the 1685 designation, 1710. Named The King's Regiment of Foot, 1713, and assigned numerical designation, 1751. Arrived at Boston June, 1774, the flank companies fighting at Lexington and Concord. Sent on the 1776 New York campaign, fighting at Long Island and Fort Washington. Sent on the 1777 Philadelphia campaign, fighting at Brandywine. Returned with the Army to New York, 1778, flank companies being sent on the Danbury, Conn., raid, then to Charleston, December, 1779. Regiment sent to East Florida, November, 1778, then to Barbadoes, July, 1779, where it spent the rest of the war. Uniform: Blue facings, lace with a blue stripe; officers' metal, silver. Today: The King's Own Royal Border Regiment.

COLONEL: General Studholme Hodgson, to 1783

Lieutenant General John Burgoyne, 1783 to war's end

COMMANDER: Colonel James Ogilvie, 1782 to war's end

LIEUTENANT COLONEL: George Maddison, to 1775

Harry Blunt, 1775-1777

James Ogilvie, 1777-1782

An officer's engraved swordbelt plate of the 4th (King's Own) Regiment of Foot. (Drawing by Rebecca Katcher)

From left, a musician, lieutenant and private of the light company, 4th (King's Own) Regiment of Foot. (Drawing by Eric Manders, courtesy of The Company of Military Historians.)

5th Regiment of Foot   Formed as a Holland Regiment, 1674 and designated 5th Regiment of Foot, 1751. Shire designation: Northumberland. Arrived at Boston July, 1774, fighting at Bunker Hill. Sent on 1776 New York campaign, fighting at Long Island, White Plains and Fort Washington. Sent on 1777 Philadelphia campaign, fighting at Brandywine and Germantown. Returned with the Army to New York, 1778, and there assigned to duty as marines aboard Admiral Byron's fleet November, 1778, ending the war in the West Indies. Uniform: Dull green facings, bastion lace with two red stripes; officers' metal, silver. Today: 1st Battalion/The Royal Regiment of Fusiliers.

> COLONEL: Lieutenant General Hugh Earl Percy
> LIEUTENANT COLONEL: William Walcott, to 1778
> William Medows, 1778-1778
> Anthony Haslam, 1777-1782
> George Harris, 1780 to war's end

6th Regiment of Foot   Formed as a Holland regiment, 1673, and thereafter known by various colonels' names until designated 6th, 1751. Shire designation: 1st Warwickshire. Arrived from St. Vincent at New York October, 1776, in sickly condition and well men transferred into other regiments while 158 officers and other ranks returned to England December, 1776. By 1778 12 companies recruited and sent to Jersey Island, 1781, and then to Ireland, 1783. Uniform: Brownish raw sienna facings, lace with a red and a yellow stripe; officers' metal, silver. Today: 2nd Battalion/The Royal Regiment of Fusiliers.

> COLONEL: General Sir William Boothby, Bt.
> LIEUTENANT COLONEL: Maurice Cane, to 1778
> Charles Home, 1778-1782
> John Whyte, 1782 to war's end

7th (Royal Fusilier) Regiment of Foot   Formed as Our Royal Regiment of Fusiliers, 1685, and redesignated 7th (Royal Fusilier) Regiment of Foot, 1751. Arrived in Quebec July, 1773. Regiment had 295 men at fall of St. Johns, 83 at fall of Chambly, 63 at defense of Quebec. Prisoners exchanged into lines at New York December, 1776, and reformed, fighting at Forts Clinton and Montgomery, 1777. Sent as reinforcements to Philadelphia, winter, 1777-1778, returning with the Army to New York, 1778, and fighting at Monmouth Court House. Sent on raids into Connecticut, 1779. Sent to Charleston December, 1779, fighting at Cowpens. While 182 men were sent to Savannah from Charleston, the rest of the regiment returned to New York August, 1782, and left for England, 1783. Uniform: Blue facings, lace with one blue stripe; officers' metal, gold. Today: 3rd Battalion/The Royal Regiment of Fusiliers.

COLONEL: Lieutenant General Robert Bertie, to 1777
Lieutenant General Richard Prescott, 1777 to war's end

COMMANDER: Colonel Alured Clarke, 1782 to war's end

LIEUTENANT COLONEL: Alured Clarke, 1777-1782

8th (King's) Regiment of Foot   Formed as Princess Anne of Denmark's Regiment of Foot, 1685, and designated The Queen's Regiment of Foot, 1702. Redesignated The King's Regiment of Foot, 1716, and given numerical designation 1751. Arrived in Canada, summer, 1768. Four companies stationed at Niagara, three at Detroit, two at Michimackinac, and one at Oswego. Fighting in raids in the Northwest, had 60 men at The Cedars and 100 at the siege of Fort Stanwix. Uniform: Blue facings, lace with a blue and a yellow stripe; officers' metal, gold. Today: The King's Regiment.

COLONEL: General Bigoe Armstrong

LIEUTENANT COLONEL: John Caldwell, to 1778
Mason Bolton, 1778-1781
Alexander Dundas, 1781 to war's end
Schuyler de Peyster, 1782 to war's end

9th Regiment of Foot   Formed in 1685, serving under various colonels' names until designated 9th, 1751. Shire designation: East Norfolk. Arrived at Quebec May, 1776, serving in operations on Lake Champlain, 1777. Part of Burgoyne's army and interned at Saratoga. Uniform: Bright yellow facings, lace with two black stripes; officers' metal, silver. Today: 1st Battalion/The Royal Anglian Regiment.

COLONEL: Lieutenant General Edward Viscount Ligonier, to 1783
Major General Thomas Lord Saye and Sele, 1783 to war's end

COMMANDER: Colonel John Hill, 1782 to war's end

LIEUTENANT COLONEL: Charles Forbes, to 1775
John Hill, 1775-1782

10th Regiment of Foot   Formed, 1685, serving under various colonels' names until given 10th designation, 1751. Shire designation: North Lincoln. Arrived at Boston October, 1774, flank companies fighting at Lexington and Concord and Bunker Hill. Sent on 1776 New York campaign, fighting at Long Island, White Plains and Fort Washington. Sent on 1776 campaign in New Jersey. Sent to Newport, R.I., November, 1776, being returned to New York and sent on 1777 Philadelphia campaign, fighting at Brandywine and Billingsport, N.J. Returned to New York with the Army, 1778. As an understrength regiment, men transferred into other regiments, while officers returned to England, 1779, where the regiment spent the rest of the war. Uniform: Bright yellow facings, lace with a blue stripe; officers' metal, silver. Today: 2nd Battalion/The Royal Anglian Regiment.

    COLONEL: Major General Edward Sanford, to 1781
               Lieutenant General Sir Robert Keith, 1781 to war's end
    COMMANDER: Major General Francis Smith, 1775 to war's end
    LIEUTENANT COLONEL: Francis Smith, to 1775
               Andrew Cathcart, 1781 to war's end

11th Regiment of Foot   Formed, 1685, serving under various colonels' names until designated 11th, 1751. Shire designation: North Devon. Served in Ireland throughout the period. Uniform: Dark green facings, bastion lace with two red stripes; officers' metal, gold. Today: The Dorsetshire and Devonshire Regiment.

    COLONEL: Lieutenant General William a'Court Ashe, to 1782
               Lieutenant General Henry Smith, 1782 to war's end
    COMMANDER: Colonel Henry Shawe, 1782 to war's end
    LIEUTENANT COLONEL: Charles Forbes, to 1776
               Henry Shawe, 1776-1782

12th Regiment of Foot   Formed, 1685, serving under various colonels' names until designated 12th, 1751. Shire designation: East Suffolk. Part of the garrison of Gibraltar during the siege. Uniform: Pale yellow facings, bastion lace with a black and a red stripe; officers' metal, gold. Today: 1st Battalion/The Royal Anglian Regiment.

    COLONEL: Major General Sir Henry Clinton, K.B., to 1778
               Major General William Picton, 1778 to war's end

13th Regiment of Foot

COMMANDER: Colonel Thomas Trigge, 1782 to war's end
LIEUTENANT COLONEL: William Picton, to 1778
Thomas Trigge, 1778-1782
Thomas Adams, 1780-1782

13th Regiment of Foot   Formed, 1685, serving under various colonels' names until designated 13th, 1751. Shire designation: 1st Somerset. Sent from Minorca to Plymouth, England, February, 1776. Sent to Barbadoes, November, 1781, returning to England, 1782. Uniform: Yellow ochre facings, lace with a yellow stripe worn in pairs; officers' metal, silver. Today: 1st Battalion/The Light Infantry.

COLONEL: Lieutenant General Hon. James Murray
COMMANDER: Colonel David Ogilvy, 1777-1781
Colonel Andrew Edhouse, 1782 to war's end
LIEUTENANT COLONEL: David Ogilvy, to 1777
Andrew Edhouse, 1777-1782

14th Regiment of Foot   Formed, 1685, serving under various colonels' names until designated 14th, 1751. Shire designation: Bedfordshire. Sent from Halifax to Boston September, 1768, then to St. Augustine and West Indies, October, 1772. Returned to Virginia, 1775, fighting at Great Bridge, Va., December, 1775. Sent to New York where, as an understrength regiment, men transferred into other regiments while officers returned to England, December, 1776. Reformed and sent to Jamaica, arriving there April, 1782, and spent the rest of the period there. Uniform: Pale buff facings, lace with a mixed red and blue stripe and a buff stripe; officers' metal, silver. Today: The Prince of Wales Own Regiment of Yorkshire.

COLONEL: Lieutenant General Hon. William Keppel, to 1776
Lieutenant General Robert Cunninghame, 1776 to war's end
COMMANDER: Colonel William Dalrymple, 1777-1780
Colonel James Rooke, 1780 to war's end
LIEUTENANT COLONEL: William Dalrymple, to 1777
Jonathan Furlong, 1777-1779
James Rooke, 1780

15th Regiment of Foot   Formed, 1685, serving under various colonels' names until designated 15th, 1751. Shire designation: East

Riding of York. Arrived from Ireland at Cape Fear, N.C., May, 1776, fighting at the first siege of Charleston. Sent to the 1776 New York campaign, fighting at Long Island and Fort Washington. Sent on 1777 Philadelphia campaign, fighting at Brandywine, Germantown and Whitemarsh. Returned with the Army to New York, 1778, fighting at Monmouth. Sent on Danbury, Conn., raid. Sent to the relief of Newport September, 1778. Returned to New York and sent on to East Florida November, 1778. From there sent to St. Kitts July, 1779, being captured there January, 1782. Uniform: Yellow ochre facings, lace with a mixed yellow and black stripe and a red stripe; officers' metal, silver. Today: The Prince of Wales Own Regiment of Yorkshire.

    COLONEL: Major General Sir C. Thompson, Bt. & K.B., to 1776
           Major General Richard Earl of Cavan, 1776-1778
           Lieutenant General William Fawcett, 1778 to war's end
    COMMANDER: Colonel Joseph Gabbett, to 1777
           Colonel Hon. Joseph Stopford, 1782 to war's end
    LIEUTENANT COLONEL: John Bird, 1776-1777
           Hugh Powell, 1777-1782
           John Maxwell, 1778-1779
           Hon. John Stopford, 1779-1782
           Henry Bruen, 1782 to war's end

16th Regiment of Foot   Formed, 1688, and served under various colonels' names until designated 16th, 1751. Shire designation: Buckinghamshire. Arrived at New York 1767, and sent to various southern posts, although a detachment returned to New York August, 1776, only to return south the next year. Regiment served at the defense of Savannah, and fall of Pensacola. One company at Port Royal Island, S.C., February, 1779, and detachment at fall of Baton Rouge, La. Returned to England where spent the rest of the period March, 1782. Uniform: Yellow ochre facings, lace with a pinkish crimson stripe; officers' metal, silver. Today: 3rd Battalion/The Royal Anglian Regiment.

    COLONEL: Major General James Gisborne, to 1779
           Lieutenant General James Robertson, 1779 to war's end
    COMMANDER: Colonel James Robertson, to 1777
           Colonel Alexander Dickson, 1782 to war's end
    LIEUTENANT COLONEL: Alexander Dickson, 1776-1782
           Colin Graham, 1783 to war's end

A silver officer's swordbelt plate of the 16th Regiment of Foot. (Drawing by Rebecca Katcher)

17th Regiment of Foot Formed 1688, serving under various colonels' names until designated 17th, 1751. Shire designation: Leicestershire. Arrived at Boston December, 1775, serving at the siege of Boston. Sent on 1776 New York campaign, fighting at Long Island and in New Jersey at Princeton. Sent on 1777 Philadelphia campaign, fighting at Brandywine, Germantown and Whitemarsh. Returned to New York with the Army, 1778, fighting at Monmouth. Sent to the relief of Newport, September, 1778. Returned to New York and sent to capture and loss of Stony Point. Sent to Virginia April, 1781, and interned at Yorktown. Exchanged and sent to Nova Scotia, 1783. Uniform: Greyish white facings, lace with two blue and one yellow stripes; officers' metal, silver. Today: 4th Battalion/The Royal Anglian Regiment.

>   COLONEL: Lieutenant General Hon. Robert Monckton, to 1783
>   Lieutenant General George Morrison, 1783 to war's end
>   COMMANDER: Colonel John Darby, to 1776
>   Colonel Henry Johnson, 1783 to war's end
>   LIEUTENANT COLONEL: Charles Mawhood, to 1778
>   Henry Johnson, 1778-1783
>   Thomas Armstrong, 1783 to war's end

18th (Royal Irish) Regiment of Foot   Formed 1684, serving under various colonels' names until designated the Royal Regiment of Ireland, 1695, and 18th (Royal Irish), 1751. Arrived at Philadelphia from Canada, 1767, although two companies remained in the Illinois country. Sent to Boston October, 1774, where flank companies fought at Lexington and Concord and Bunker Hill. As an understrength regiment, men transferred to other regiments, while officers returned to British Isles where regiment spent the rest of the period. Uniform: Blue facings, lace with a blue stripe; officers' metal, gold. Regiment disbanded, 1922.

COLONEL: General Sir John Sebright, Bt.
COMMANDER: Colonel Sir Alexander Purves, Bt., 1780 to war's end
Colonel Adam Williamson, 1782 to war's end
(also served as the Army Deputy Adjutant General)
LIEUTENANT COLONEL: John Wilkins, to 1775
Adam Williamson, 1775-1782
Sir Alexander Purves, Bt., 1780-1780

19th Regiment of Foot   Formed 1688, serving under various colonels' names until designated 19th, 1751. Shire designation: North Riding of York. Sent from Cork, Ireland, to Charleston June, 1781, and sent to the relief of Ninety Six. Regimental baggage lost at Monks Corner, S.C., July, 1781, and flank companies fought at Eutaw Springs. Sent from Charleston to St. Croix and Antigua December, 1782, and then to St. Lucia where it spent the rest of the period. Uniform: Dark brownish green facings, lace with a mixed red and green stripe and a red and a green stripe; officers' metal, gold. Today: The Green Howards (Princess Alexandra's Own Yorkshire Regiment).

COLONEL: General David Graeme
COMMANDER: Colonel James Coates, 1782 to war's end
LIEUTENANT COLONEL: James Coates, 1775-1782

20th Regiment of Foot   Formed 1688, serving under various colonels' names until designated 20th, 1751. Shire designation: East Devonshire. Arrived for the relief of Quebec May, 1776. Served in the Burgoyne campaign and interned at Saratoga. Uniform: Pale yellow facings, lace with a black and a red stripe in pairs; officers' metal, silver. Today: 4th Battalion/The Royal Regiment of Fusiliers (Disbanded).

COLONEL: Lieutenant General Hon. George Lane Parker, to 1782
Major General William Wynyard, 1782 to war's end
COMMANDER: Colonel John Lind, 1782 to war's end
LIEUTENANT COLONEL: John Parr, to 1776
John Lind, 1776-1782

An engraved brass belt plate of the 20th Regiment of Foot. (Drawing by Rebecca Katcher)

21st Regiment of Foot (Royal North British Fusiliers)

Formed as Colonel the Earl of Mar's Regiment of Foot, although also known as The Scots Fusiliers Regiment of Foot, 1678, and designated the Scots Fusilier Regiment of Foot, 1707. Redesignated The Royal North British Fusiliers Regiment of Foot, 1712, and assigned number, 1751. Arrived for the relief of Quebec May, 1776, serving on operations on Lake Champlain, 1776. Served in the Burgoyne campaign and interned at Saratoga. Uniform: Blue facings, lace with a blue stripe; officers' metal, gold. Today: The Royal Highland Fusiliers.

COLONEL: Lieutenant General Hon. Alexander Mackay
COMMANDER: Colonel James Hamilton, 1780 to war's end
LIEUTENANT COLONEL: James Hamilton, to 1780
George Forster, 1782 to war's end

22nd Regiment of Foot   Formed 1689, serving under various colonels' names until designated 22nd, 1751. Shire designation: Cheshire. Arrived at Boston July, 1775, serving in that city's siege. Sent on 1776 New York campaign, fighting at Long Island. Sent to Newport November, 1776. Returned to New York, fighting at Springfield, N.J., 1780. Returned to England, 1783. Uniform: Pale buff facings, bastion lace with a red and a blue stripe in pairs; officers' metal, gold. Today: The Cheshire Regiment.

    COLONEL: Lieutenant General Hon. Thomas Gage, to 1782
              Major General Charles O'Hara, 1782 to war's end
    LIEUTENANT COLONEL: James Abercromby, to 1776
              John Campbell, 1776-1778
              Rawlins Hilman, 1777-1779
              John Yorke, 1778-1782
              William Crosbie, 1780 to war's end
              William Crowley, 1783 to war's end

23rd Regiment of Foot (Royal Welch Fusiliers)   Formed as Colonel Lord Herbert's Regiment of Foot, 1688, and designated The Prince of Wales Own Royal Regiment of Welch Fusiliers, 1714. Designated The Royal Welch Fusiliers, 1727, and numerical designation added 1751. Arrived at New York June, 1773, and sent to Boston, 1775, to serve in the siege there. Sent on the 1776 New York campaign, fighting at Long Island, White Plains and Fort Washington. Sent on the 1777 Philadelphia campaign, fighting at Brandywine and Germantown. Returned with the Army to New York, 1778, fighting at Monmouth Court House. Sent as marines on the fleet off Newport, July-September, 1778. Participated in Danbury, Conn., raid, 1780, and capture of Stony Point. Sent to Charleston, December, 1779, fighting in that city's siege, Camden, Polk's Mill, Catawba Crossing, Guilford Court House and interned at Yorktown. Detachment in Charleston sent to Halifax November, 1782. Uniform: Blue facings, lace with a red, a blue and a yellow stripe; officers' metal, gold. Today: The Royal Welsh Fusiliers.[5]

    COLONEL: Lieutenant General Hon. George Boseawen, to 1775
              Lieutenant General Sir William Howe, K.B., 1775 to war's end
    LIEUTENANT COLONEL: Benjamin Bernard, to 1778
              William Blakeney, 1778-1780
              Nesbitt Balfour, 1778-1783
              Richard Temple, 1783 to war's end

A squad of the reconstructed 23rd (Royal Welch Fusiliers) shows the uniform in the field of a typical British unit. A sergeant is on the left, carring his Brown Bess at "advance." (Photograph by Arthur Blundell, courtesy *Soldier* Magazine.)

A private of the light company, 23rd (Royal Welch Fusiliers) after Bunker Hill. The original company was virtually destroyed and a new company was created from among battalion men. His hat is made from an ordinary battalion cap, re-cut, and his long coat shortened. His accoutrements are also standard battalion ones. (Drawing by George C. Woodbridge, courtesy of the *Brigade Dispatch.*)

24th Regiment of Foot   Formed 1689, serving under various colonels' names until designated 24th, 1751. Shire designation: 2nd Warwickshire. Arrived for the relief of Quebec May, 1776, serving on operations on Lake Champlain, 1776. Served on the Burgoyne campaign and interned at Saratoga. Uniform: A very dark bluish green facing color, lace with a red and a green stripe; officers' metal, silver. Today: The Royal Regiment of Wales.

COLONEL: Lieutenant General Hon. Edward Cornwallis, to 1777
Lieutenant General William Tayler, 1777 to war's end
LIEUTENANT COLONEL: Simon Fraser, to 1777
Alexander Earl of Balcarres, 1777-1782
William Agnew, 1782-1783
Richard England, 1783 to war's end

25th Regiment of Foot   Formed as The Edinburgh Regiment of Foot, 1689, and designated 25th, 1751. Shire designation: Sussex. Sent from England to the relief of Gibraltar October, 1782, where it finished the war. Uniform: Yellow ochre facings, bastion lace with a blue, a red and a yellow stripe; officers' metal, gold. Today: The King's Own Scottish Borderers.

COLONEL: Lieutenant General Lord George H. Lennox
COMMANDER: Colonel Alexander Rigby, 1780 to war's end
LIEUTENANT COLONEL: Alexander Rigby, to 1780
A. Fotheringham Ogilvie, 1777-1779

26th Regiment of Foot (Cameronians)   Formed 1689, serving both under various colonels' names as well as the name of The Cameronians until designated 26th, 1751. Arrived at New Jersey summer, 1767, and sent to Canada April, 1775. Companies stationed at Montreal, Trois Rivieres, Chambly, St. Johns, Ticonderoga and Crown Point. Captured at the fall of St. Johns and exchanged December, 1776. Sent to New York, fighting in the 1777 Jersey campaign and Forts Clinton and Montgomery. Sent as reinforcements to Philadelphia, 1777, returning with the Army to New York, 1778, fighting at Monmouth Court House. As an understrength regiment, men transferred to other regiments and officers returned to British Isles to recruit, December, 1779, where unit spent the rest of the period. Uniform: Pale yellow facings, lace with two yellow and one blue stripe; officers' metal, silver. Today: The Cameronians (Scottish Rifles) (Disbanded May, 1968)

COLONEL: Major General John Scott, to 1775

Major General Lord Adam Gordon, 1775-1783

Major General Sir William Erskine, Kt, 1783 to war's end

COMMANDER: Colonel Hon. Charles Stuart, 1782 to war's end

LIEUTENANT COLONEL: Dudley Templer, to 1777

Hon. Charles Stuart, 1777-1782

27th Regiment of Foot (Enniskillings)   Formed 1689, serving under various colonels' names until designated 27th (Enniskillings), 1751. Arrived at Boston, October, 1775, serving in the siege there. Sent on the 1776 New York campaign, fighting at Long Island and Fort Washington. Sent on the 1777 Philadelphia campaign, fighting at Brandywine and Germantown. Returned to New York, 1777, fighting at Quintan's Bridge, N.J., 1778, and on the Danbury, Conn., raid. Sent to East Florida November, 1778, and then to St. Lucia where the unit finished the war. Uniform: Pale buff facings, lace with a blue and a red stripe worn in pairs; officers' metal, gold. Today: 1st Battalion/The Royal Irish Rangers.

COLONEL: Major General Eyre Massey

LIEUTENANT COLONEL: John Beckwith, to 1775

John Maxwell, 1775-1777

Edward Mitchell, 1777-1780

Joseph Ferguson, 1780 to war's end

28th Regiment of Foot   Formed 1694, serving under various colonels' names until designated 28th, 1751. Shire designation: Gloucestershire. Arrived from Cork at Cape Fear, N.C., May, 1776, serving at the first siege of Charleston. Sent on the 1776 New York campaign, fighting at Long Island and Fort Washington. Sent on the 1777 Philadelphia campaign, fighting at Brandywine and Germantown. Returned with the Army to New York, 1778, and sent from there to East Florida November, 1778. Left there for St. Kitts July, 1779, where captured January, 1782. Uniform: Bright yellow facings, lace with one yellow and two black stripes; officers' metal, silver. Today: The Gloucestershire Regiment.

COLONEL: Major General Thomas Earle, to 1778

29th Regiment of Foot

Lieutenant General Sir Charles Grey, K.B., 1778 to war's end

COMMANDER: Colonel Robert Prescott, 1777-1780

Colonel Robert Kingston, 1782 to war's end

LIEUTENANT COLONEL: Arthur Brown, to 1776

Robert Prescott, 1775-1777

Robert Kingston, 1782

An engraved swordbelt plate of the 28th Regiment of Foot. (Drawing by Rebecca Katcher)

29th Regiment of Foot　　　Formed 1694, serving under various colonels' names until designated 29th, 1751. Shire designation: Worcestershire. Sent from Halifax to Boston September, 1768, participating in the "Boston Massacre," March, 1770. Sent to the relief of Quebec May, 1776, and stationed in Canada throughout the period. Flank companies on Burgoyne expedition and interned at Saratoga. Uniform: Yellow ochre facings, bastion lace with two blue and one yellow stripes; officers' metal, silver. Today: The Worcestershire & Sherwood Foresters Regiment.

COLONEL: Lieutenant General William Evelyn

COMMANDER: Colonel Thomas Carleton, 1782 to war's end

LIEUTENANT COLONEL: Maurice Carr, to 1776

Thomas Carleton, 1776-1782

Christopher Carleton, 1783 to war's end

From left, a sergeant holding a halberd, a grenadier, an officer, a Negro drummer, and a pioneer of the 29th Regiment of Foot in Boston just prior to the outbreak of war. (Drawing by Peter Copeland, courtesy of The Company of Military Historians.)

30th Regiment of Foot   Formed 1714, serving under various colonels' names until designated 30th, 1751. Shire designation: Cambridgeshire. Sent from Cork to Charleston June, 1781, and then to the relief of Ninety Six. Flank companies at Eutaw Springs. Left for Antigua and St. Croix, and then to St. Lucia December, 1782. Uniform: Pale yellow facings, bastion lace with a pale blue stripe; officers' metal, silver. Today: The Queen's Lancashire Regiment.

COLONEL: General John Parslow
COMMANDER: Colonel Paston Gould, 1777-1782
LIEUTENANT COLONEL: Paston Gould, to 1777
    Christopher Maxwell, 1782 to war's end
    John Augustus Jevers, 1783 to war's end

31st Regiment of Foot   Formed 1713, serving under various colonels' names until designated 31st, 1751. Shire designation: Huntingdonshire. Sent from West Indies to the relief of Quebec May, 1776, serving in operations on Lake Champlain. Stationed in Canada throughout the period, although flank companies on Burgoyne expedition and interned at Saratoga. Uniform: Buff facings, lace with a yellow and blue worm and a red stripe; officers' metal, silver. Today: 1st Battalion/The Queen's Regiment.

COLONEL: Lieutenant General James A. Oughton, K.B., to 1780
    Lieutenant General Thomas Clarke, 1780 to war's end
COMMANDER: Colonel Jeremiah French, 1782 to war's end
LIEUTENANT COLONEL: Alexander Mackenzie, to 1777
    Jeremiah French, 1777-1782

32nd Regiment of Foot   Formed as marines 1702, and made a foot regiment 1714, serving under various colonels' names until designated 32nd, 1751. Shire designation: Cornwall. Sent from England to Ireland, 1775, on H.M.S. Rockingham, which was wrecked off the coast with loss of 90 men and much regimental property. Stationed in Cork and Dublin until sent to Gibraltar, 1783. Uniform: White facings, lace with a black worm and a black stripe; officers' metal, gold. Today: 1st Battalion/The Light Infantry.

COLONEL: Colonel Robert Robinson, to 1776
    Major General William Amherst, 1776-1780
    Major General Robert Earl of Ross, 1780 to war's end
COMMANDER: Major General John Fletcher Campbell, to war's end

LIEUTENANT COLONEL: John Fletcher Campbell, to 1777
Edmund Strachan, 1782 to war's end

33rd Regiment of Foot   Formed 1702, serving under various colonels' names until designated 33rd, 1751. Shire designation: 1st Yorkshire West Riding. Sent from West Indies to Cape Fear, N.C., May, 1776, fighting at the first siege of Charleston. Sent on the 1776 New York campaign, fighting at Long Island, Harlem Heights and Fort Washington. Sent on the 1777 Philadelphia campaign, fighting at Brandywine, Germantown and Whitemarsh. Returned to New York with the Army, 1778, fighting at Monmouth Court House. Sent to the relief of Newport September, 1778. Returned to New York, fighting at Old Tappen, N.Y. Sent to the second siege of Charleston, December, 1779, fighting at Camden, Charlotte, Wetzell's Mills, Guilford Court House, Green Spring, Va., and interned at Yorktown. Detachment at Charleston sent to Halifax November, 1782, where rest of the regiment joined them September, 1783. Uniform: Red facings, bastion lace with a red stripe; officers' metal, silver. Today: The Duke of Wellington's West Riding Regiment.

COLONEL: Lieutenant General Charles Earl Cornwallis
COMMANDER: Colonel John Yorke, 1783 to war's end
LIEUTENANT COLONEL: James Webster, to 1780
John Yorke, 1782-1783

34th Regiment of Foot   Formed 1702, serving under various colonels' names until designated 34th, 1751. Shire designation: Cumberland. Arrived for the relief of Quebec May, 1776, and stationed in Canada throughout the period, although flank companies served on Burgoyne campaign and interned at Saratoga. Uniform: Bright yellow facings, lace with a blue and yellow worm and a red stripe worn in pairs; officers' metal, silver. Today: The King's Own Royal Border Regiment.

COLONEL: Lieutenant General Lord Frederick Cavendish
COMMANDER: Colonel Barry St. Ledger, 1780 to war's end
LIEUTENANT COLONEL: Samuel Townsend, to 1776
Barry St. Ledger, 1776-1780
Robert Hoyes, 1783 to war's end

35th Regiment of Foot   Formed 1701, serving under various colonels' names until designated 35th, 1751. Shire designation: Dorsetshire. Arrived at Boston June, 1775, flank companies fighting at Bunker Hill. Sent on 1776 New York campaign, fighting at Long Island and White Plains. Sent from New York to St. Lucia, November, 1778, where spent the rest of the war. Uniform: Officially orange facings, but actually a brownish yellow, lace with a yellow stripe; officers' metal, silver. Today: 3rd Battalion/The Queen's Regiment.

COLONEL: Lieutenant General Henry Fletcher Campbell
LIEUTENANT COLONEL: Hon. Richard Allen, to 1775
Robert Carr, 1775-1777
Hon. Lockhart Gordon, 1777-1780
James Cockburne, 1778 to war's end

36th Regiment of Foot   Formed 1702, serving under various colonels' names until designated 36th, 1751. Shire designation: Herefordshire. Sent from England to Ireland September, 1775. Returned from Ireland and sent to Madras, India, March, 1782, arriving there July, 1782, and fighting at the capture of Cannonore December, 1782. Uniform: Dull dark green facings, lace with a red and a green stripe; officers' metal, gold. Today: The Worcestershire & Sherwood Foresters.

COLONEL: Lieutenant General Richard Pierson, to 1779 Major
Gen. Hon. Henry St. John, 1779 to war's end
COMMANDER: Colonel Thomas Calcraft, to 1777
Brevet Major General Allan Campbell, 1783 to war's end
LIEUTENANT COLONEL: Allan Campbell, to 1780

37th Regiment of Foot   Formed 1702, serving under various colonels' names until designated 37th, 1751. Shire designation: North Hampshire. Arrived at Cape Fear, N.C., from Cork, May, 1776, fighting at the first siege of Charleston. Sent on the 1776 New York campaign, fighting at Long Island. Sent on the 1777 Jersey campaign. Sent on the 1777 Philadelphia campaign, fighting at Brandywine and Germantown. Returned to New York with the Army, 1778, fighting at Monmouth Court House. Sent to the relief of Newport September, 1778. Returned to New York and 13 companies sent to St. Augustine, Florida, while the rest of the unit went to Nova

In the foreground, left, are a musician and a sergeant of the 35th Regiment of Foot, while in the background are a light company and a battalion man. (Drawing by Eric Manders, courtesy of The Company of Military Historians.)

38th Regiment of Foot

Scotia September, 1779, where the unit spent the rest of the period. Uniform: Bright yellow facings, lace with a red and a yellow stripe; officers' metal, silver. Today: The Royal Hampshire Regiment.

COLONEL: Lieutenant General Sir Eyre Coote, K.B.

LIEUTENANT COLONEL: John Pennington, to 1775

Robert Abercromby, 1775-1777

James Cousseau, 1780-1782

A rather plain, engraved waistbelt plate of the 37th Regiment of Foot. (Drawing by Rebecca Katcher)

38th Regiment of Foot   Formed 1705, serving under various colonels' names until designated 38th, 1751. Shire designation: 1st Staffordshire. Arrived at Boston July, 1774, flank companies fighting at Lexington and Concord. Unit at Bunker Hill and the siege of Boston. Sent on the 1777 Jersey campaign. Sent to the defense of Newport, July, 1778. Returned to New York, fighting at Springfield, N.J., and the raid on New London, Conn. Returned to England, 1783. Uniform: Bright yellow facings, bastion lace with two red stripes and one yellow stripe; officers' metal, silver. Today: The Staffordshire Regiment.

COLONEL: Major General Sir Robert Pigot, Bt.

LIEUTENANT COLONEL: William Butler, 1775-1778

Hon. Henry F. Fox, 1778-1783

William Handfield, 1783 to war's end

An engraved swordbelt plate of the 38th Regiment of Foot. (Drawing by Rebecca Katcher)

39th Regiment of Foot　　　Formed 1702, serving under various colonels' names until designated 39th, 1751. Shire designation: East Middlesex. Served in the garrison of Gibraltar during the siege. Uniform: Dull lightish green facings, lace with a green stripe; officers' metal, gold. Today: The Dorsetshire & Devonshire Regiment.
　　COLONEL: Lieutenant General Robert Boyd
　　COMMANDER: Colonel William Kellett, 1782 to war's end
　　LIEUTENANT COLONEL: Charles Ross, to 1777
　　　　　　　　　　　　William Kellett, 1777-1782
　　　　　　　　　　　　John Freke, 1783 to war's end

40th Regiment of Foot　　　Formed 1717, serving under various colonels' names until designated 40th, 1751. Shire designation: 2nd Somersetshire. Arrived at Boston June, 1775, serving in the siege there. Sent on the 1776 New York campaign, fighting at Long Island and Princeton. Sent on the 1777 Philadelphia campaign, fighting at Brandywine, Paoli and Germantown. Returned with the Army to New York, 1778. Sent to East Florida November, 1778. Six companies sent to Antigua July, 1779, while the rest of the regiment went to Barbadoes. Served as marines aboard Admiral Sir Samuel Hood's fleet. Returned to New York August, 1781, serving on the

41st Regiment of Foot

New London, Conn., raid. Returned to England, 1783. Uniform: Buff facings, lace with a black and a red stripe; officers' metal, gold. Today: The Queen's Lancashire Regiment.

COLONEL: Lieutenant General Sir Robert Hamilton, Bt.
COMMANDER: Colonel James Grant, to 1776
LIEUTENANT COLONEL: James Grant, 1775-1778
Thomas Musgrave, 1778-1782
John G. Simcoe, 1781-1783
Edmund Eyre, 1783 to war's end

41st Regiment of Foot   Formed as independent companies of invalids 1719, and regimented as the 41st Regiment of Invalids, 1751. Served throughout the war in the British Isles, being made up of soldiers unable to serve in active regiments. Uniform: Blue facings, no lace but blue stitched button holes; officers' metal, gold. Today: The Royal Regiment of Wales.

COLONEL: Lieutenant General Gordon Wren
COMMANDER: Major General Archibald McNab, 1777 to war's end
Colonel William Roberts, 1782 to war's end
LIEUTENANT COLONEL: Archibald McNab, to 1777
William Roberts, to 1782

42nd Regiment of Foot (Royal Highland Regiment)   Formed as The Highland Regiment, 1739, and designated the 42nd, 1751. Received Royal designation 1758. Arrived at New York July, 1776, fighting at Long Island, Harlem Heights and Fort Washington. Served on 1777 Jersey campaign. Sent on the 1777 Philadelphia campaign, fighting at Brandywine, Paoli, Billingsport, N.J., and Whitemarsh. Returned with the Army to New York, 1778, fighting at Monmouth Court House. Sent to the relief of Newport September, 1778. Sent from there to East Florida November, 1778. Sent to Charleston for the siege December, 1779, and then on the raid on Portsmouth, Va., 1780. Returned to Charleston and then sent to New York and on to Halifax September, 1783. Second battalion formed and sent to Bombay May, 1781, fighting at Coondapoor January, 1783. Second battalion redesignated 73rd Regiment of Foot March, 1786. Uniform: Blue facings, bastion lace with one red stripe; officers' metal, gold; Highland kilts and bonnets. Today: The Black Watch.

COLONEL: General Lord John Murray
LIEUTENANT COLONEL: Thomas Sterling, to 1778
Duncan McPherson, 1777-1781
William Grant, 1777-1779
Norman MacLeod, 1780 to war's end
Charles Graham, 1782 to war's end

43rd Regiment of Foot   Formed 1741, serving under various colonels' names until designated 43rd, 1751. Shire designation: Monmouthshire. Arrived at Boston July, 1774, flank companies fighting at Lexington and Concord, while whole regiment fought at Bunker Hill. Sent on the 1776 New York campaign, fighting at Long Island and Fort Washington. Sent to Newport November, 1776. Returned to New York and took part in raids into New Jersey, 1781. Sent to Virginia, April, 1781, fighting at Greenspring and interned at Yorktown. Uniform: White facings, lace with a red and a black stripe; officers' metal, silver. Today: 1st Battalion/The Royal Green Jackets.

COLONEL: General Hon. George Cary
COMMANDER: Colonel James Marsh, 1782 to war's end
LIEUTENANT COLONEL: George Clerk, 1776-1778
James Marsh, 1778-1782

44th Regiment of Foot   Formed 1741, serving under various colonels' names until designated 44th, 1751. Shire designation: East Essex. Arrived at Boston June, 1775. Flank companies sent to first siege of Charleston. Regiment sent on 1776 New York campaign, fighting at Long Island. Sent on 1777 Philadelphia campaign, fighting at Brandywine, Paoli, Germantown and Whitemarsh. Returned with the Army to New York, 1778, fighting at Monmouth Court House. Sent on Danbury, Conn., raid, and to the relief of Newport, September, 1778. Sent to Canada September, 1779, finally reaching Quebec after losing many men in stormy seas June, 1780, where they spent the rest of the war. Uniform: Bright yellow facings, lace with a black, a yellow and a blue stripe; officers' metal, silver. Today: 3rd Battalion/The Royal Anglian Regiment.

COLONEL: Lieutenant General James Abercromby, to 1780
Lieutenant General Charles Rainsford, 1780 to war's end

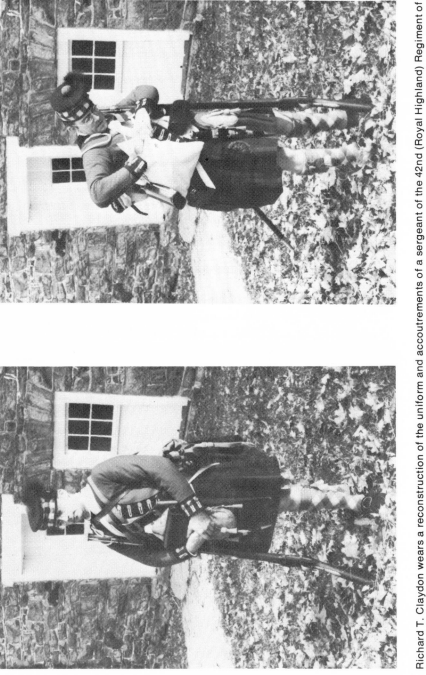

Richard T. Claydon wears a reconstruction of the uniform and accoutrements of a sergeant of the 42nd (Royal Highland) Regiment of Foot. For dress, the Regiment's sergeants wore rectangular silver lace, instead of plain white or bastion lace. They also carried their broadswords, while the men gave up theirs upon arriving in New York in 1776. Officers and sergeants of Highland regiments wore their sashes across their bodies, not around their waists.

COMMANDER: Colonel Henry Hope, 1782 to war's end
LIEUTENANT COLONEL: James Agnew, to 1775
Robert Donkin, 1777-1779
Henry Hope, 1777-1782

45th Regiment of Foot   Formed 1741, serving under various colonels' names until designated 45th, 1751. Shire designation: Nottinghamshire. Arrived at Boston July, 1775. Sent on 1776 New York campaign, fighting at Long Island. As an understrength regiment, men transferred to other regiments while officers returned to the British Isles where the regiment spent the rest of the war. Uniform: Dark bluish green facings, bastion lace with a green worm; officers' metal, silver. Today: The Worcestershire and Sherwood Foresters.

COLONEL: General William Haviland
COMMANDER: Colonel James Cunninghame, to 1776
LIEUTENANT COLONEL: Hon. Henry Monckton, to 1778
William Gardiner, 1778-1783
Hon. Henry Phipps, 1783 to war's end
Henry Knight, 1783 to war's end
Horatio A. Powlet, 1783 to war's end

46th Regiment of Foot   Raised 1741, serving under various colonels' names until designated 46th, 1751. Shire designation: Cornwall. Arrived at Cape Fear, N.C., from Cork May, 1776, fighting at the first siege of Charleston. Sent on 1776 New York campaign, fighting at Long Island. Sent on 1777 Philadelphia campaign, fighting at Brandywine and Germantown. Returned with the Army to New York, 1778, fighting at Monmouth Court House and Quintan's Bridge, N.J. Sent to the relief of Newport September, 1778. Returned to New York and sent as marines on Admiral Byron's fleet November, 1778, finishing the war in the West Indies. Uniform: Pale yellow facings, lace with one red and one purple stripe; officers' metal, silver. Today: 1st Battalion/The Light Infantry.

COLONEL: Lieutenant General Sir William Howe, K.B., to 1776
Lieutenant General Hon. John Vaughan, 1776 to war's end
COMMANDER: Colonel Hon. John Vaughan, to 1776
Colonel Enoch Markham, 1780 to war's end
LIEUTENANT COLONEL: Enoch Markham, 1775-1780

47th Regiment of Foot   Formed 1741, serving under various colonels' names until designated 47th, 1751. Shire designation: Lancashire. Arrived at New Jersey 1773 and sent to Boston October, 1774. Served on relief column, Lexington and Concord and fought at Bunker Hill. Sent to the relief of Quebec March, 1776, serving in operations on Lake Champlain. Sent on Burgoyne campaign and interned at Saratoga. Uniform: White facings, lace with one red stripe between two black stripes; officers' metal, silver. Today: The Queen's Lancashire Regiment.

COLONEL: Lieutenant General Sir Guy Carleton, K.B.

LIEUTENANT COLONEL: William Nesbitt, to 1778
Nicholas Sutherland, 1778-1782
William Sherriffe, 1780-1782
Paul A. Irving, 1780 to war's end

48th Regiment of Foot   Formed 1741, serving under various colonels' names until designated 48th, 1751. Shire designation: Northamptonshire. In West Indies at war's start, a detachment at Dominica being captured September, 1778. Returned to England, 1781, and sent to Ireland October, 1783. Uniform: Buff facings, lace with one red and one black stripe; officers' metal, gold. Today: 2nd Battalion/The Royal Anglian Regiment.

COLONEL: Lieutenant General William A. Sorell, to 1783
Lieutenant General Robert Skene, 1783 to war's end

COMMANDER: Major General Benjamin Gordon, 1779 to war's end

LIEUTENANT COLONEL: Benjamin Gordon, to 1779
William Edmestone, 1777-1782
Joseph French, 1777-1779
Sir James Cockburne, Bt., 1777-1780
John Hedges, 1783 to war's end

49th Regiment of Foot   Founded 1743, serving under various colonels' names until designated 49th, 1751. Shire designation: Hertfordshire. Arrived at Boston June, 1775. Sent on 1776 New York campaign, fighting at Long Island, White Plains and Fort Washington. Sent on 1777 Philadelphia campaign, fighting at Brandywine and Germantown. Returned with the Army to New York, 1778, and sent to St. Lucia that November where it finished the war. Uniform: Very dark blue green facings, bastion lace with two red and one green stripe; officers' metal, gold. Today: The Duke of Edinburgh's Royal Regiment.

COLONEL: Lieutenant General Alexander Maitland

COMMANDER: Major General Sir Henry Calder, Bt., 1778 to war's end

LIEUTENANT COLONEL: Sir Henry Calder, Bt., to 1778
William Browne, 1782 to war's end

Marines   In 1755 50 companies of marines permanently established. In America marines served on the relief column at Lexington and Concord, Bunker Hill, Fort Washington, the relief of Quebec and the siege of Newport. All marines recalled to the Home Fleet March, 1778, although marines were in the garrison of Gibraltar during the siege. Uniform: White facings, lace with a red and a blue stripe; officers' metal, silver. Today: The Royal Marines.

50th Regiment of Foot   Formed as the 52nd Regiment of Foot 1755, and renumbered 1757. Shire designation: West Kent. Arrived from West Indies to New York July, 1776, but men quite sickly and well men transferred to other regiments August, 1776, while officers and sick men returned to Salisbury, England, November, 1776. Regiment reformed and sent aboard the H.M.SS. Centaur, Vengeance, Defiance, Thunderer and Vigilance as marines during the naval actions off Ushant July, 1778. Afterwards, returned to Exeter, England where spent the rest of the period. Reduced from ten to eight companies June, 1783. Uniform: Black facings, lace with one red stripe worn in pairs; officers' metal, silver. Today: 2nd Battalion/The Queen's Regiment.[6]

COLONEL: Lieutenant General Michael O. Dilkes, to 1776
Colonel Hon. George Monson, 1776-1778
Lieutenant General Sir Thomas S. Wilson, Bt., 1778 to war's end

COMMANDER: Colonel John Dalling, to 1777

LIEUTENANT COLONEL: John Gordon, 1776-1783
William Edmeston, 1782-1783
John Shee, 1783 to war's end

This officer's coat of the 49th Regiment of Foot is seemingly typical in design of all British and most Provincials during the period. (Courtesy of the National Army Museum.)

51st Regiment of Foot　　Formed as the 53rd Regiment of Foot 1755 and renumbered 1757. Shire designation: 2nd Yorkshire, West Riding. Served in the garrison of Minorca, surrendering there February, 1782, and returning to England May, 1782. Uniform: Olive green facings, bastion lace with a green stripe; officers' metal, gold. Today: 2nd Battalion/The Light Infantry.

　　COLONEL: Lieutenant General Archibald Earl of Eglinton
　　COMMANDER: Major General Henry Pringle, 1779 to war's end
　　LIEUTENANT COLONEL: Henry Pringle, to 1779
　　　　　　　　Andrew de la Cour, 1777-1779

52nd Regiment of Foot　　Formed as the 54th Regiment of Foot 1755 and renumbered 1757. Shire designation: Oxfordshire. Arrived at Boston October, 1774, the flank companies fighting at Lexington and Concord. Regiment fought at Bunker Hill. Sent on the 1776 New York campaign, fighting at Long Island and Fort Washington. Sent on the 1777 Jersey campaign. Sent to the relief of Newport November, 1776. Returned to New York and, as an understrength regiment, men transferred to other regiments while officers returned to British Isles where spent the rest of the war, August, 1778. Uniform: Buff facings, lace with a red worm and an orange stripe; officers' metal, silver. Today: 1st Battalion/The Royal Green Jackets.

　　COLONEL: Lieutenant General John Clavering, to 1779
　　　　　　　General Cyrus Trapaud, 1779 to war's end
　　COMMANDER: Colonel Valentine Jones, to 1777
　　　　　　　Colonel Turner Straubenzee, 1783 to war's end
　　　　　　　Colonel William Ogle, 1782 to war's end
　　LIEUTENANT COLONEL: Mungo Campbell, 1776-1777
　　　　　　　　William Ogle, 1779-1782
　　　　　　　　Christopher French, 1777-1778
　　　　　　　　Hon. John Gordon, 1777-1778
　　　　　　　　Turner Straubenzee, 1778-1783

53rd Regiment of Foot　　Formed as the 55th Regiment of Foot 1755 and renumbered 1757. Shire designation: Shropshire. Sent to the relief of Quebec May, 1776, and served in the Burgoyne campaign, being interned at Saratoga, although some of the regiment remained in Canada throughout the war. Uniform: Red facings, lace with a red stripe; officers' metal, gold. Today: 3rd Battalion/The Light Infantry.

54th Regiment of Foot

> COLONEL: Lieutenant General H.D. Horn Elphinstone
> COMMANDER: Major General Henry Watson Powell, 1779 to war's end
> LIEUTENANT COLONEL: Henry Watson Powell, to 1779
> John Nairne, 1783 to war's end

54th Regiment of Foot   Formed as the 56th Regiment of Foot 1755 and renumbered 1757. Shire designation: West Norfolk. Arrived from Cork at Cape Fear, N.C., May, 1776, fighting at first siege of Charleston. Sent on the 1776 New York campaign, fighting at Long Island. Sent to Newport November, 1776. Returned to New York June, 1779, and sent on raids into Connecticut, 1779, and New London. Conn., raid. Sent to Halifax September, 1782. Uniform: Dull yellowish green facings, lace with a green stripe; officers' metal, silver. Today: The Devonshire & Dorsetshire Regiment.

> COLONEL: Lieutenant General Mariscoe Frederick
> COMMANDER: Colonel Andrew Bruce, 1782 to war's end
> LIEUTENANT COLONEL: Robert Walsh, to 1775
> Alured Clarke, 1775-1777
> Andrew Bruce, 1777-1782
> Edmund Dyre, 1782 to war's end

55th Regiment of Foot   Formed as the 57th Regiment of Foot 1755 and renumbered 1757. Shire designation: Westmoreland. Arrived at Boston December, 1775. Sent on 1776 New York campaign, fighting at Long Island and Princeton. Sent on 1777 Philadelphia campaign, fighting at Brandywine and Germantown. Returned with the Army to New York, 1778, and sent to East Florida that November. Sent then to St. Kitts July, 1779, where captured January, 1782. Uniform: Very dark blue green facings, lace with two green stripes; officers' metal, gold. Today: The King's Own Royal Border Regiment.

> COLONEL: Major General Richard Earl of Cavan, to 1776
> Lieutenant General James Grant, 1776 to war's end
> COMMANDER: Colonel Cornelius Cuyler, 1782 to war's end
> Colonel Normand Lamont, 1782 to war's end
> LIEUTENANT COLONEL: Francis Legge, to 1776
> William Medows, 1776-1777
> Cornelius Cuyler, 1777-1782
> Normand Lamont, 1777-1782

56th Regiment of Foot   Formed as the 58th Regiment of Foot 1755 and renumbered 1757. Shire designation: East Essex. Part of the garrison of Gibraltar during the siege. Uniform: Facings officially purple but actually a very dark violet, lace with a pink stripe; officers' metal, silver. Today: 3rd Battalion/The Royal Anglian Regiment.

    COLONEL: Lieutenant General Hunt Walsh
    COMMANDER: Colonel Peter Craig, 1782 to war's end
    LIEUTENANT COLONEL: Alexander Moneypenny, to 1776
                     John Caulfield, 1776-1778
                     Peter Craig, 1778-1782
                     Bulleine Fancourt, 1782 to war's end
                     John Barker, 1783 to war's end
                     John Hardy, 1783 to war's end
                     John Hallowes, 1783 to war's end

57th Regiment of Foot   Formed as the 59th Regiment of Foot 1755 and renumbered 1757. Shire designation: West Middlesex. Arrived from Cork at Cape May, N.C., May, 1776, fighting in the first siege of Charleston. Sent on the 1776 New York campaign, fighting at Long Island. Stationed in that city until sent to Halifax September, 1783. Uniform: Bright yellow facings, lace with a black stripe; officers' metal, gold. Today: 4th Battalion/The Queen's Regiment.

    COLONEL: Lieutenant General Sir John Irvine, K.B., to 1781
              Major General John Campbell, 1781 to war's end
    COMMANDER: Colonel John Campbell, 1777-1781
    LIEUTENANT COLONEL: John Campbell, to 1777
                     Robert McLeroth, 1780-1783
                     Charles Brownlos, 1782 to war's end

58th Regiment of Foot   Formed as the 60th Regiment of Foot 1755 and renumbered 1757. Shire designation: Rutlandshire. Part of the garrison of Gibraltar during the siege. Uniform: Black facings, lace with a red stripe; officers' metal, gold. Today: 2nd Battalion/The Royal Anglian Regiment.

    COLONEL: Major General Robert Cunninghame, to 1776
              Colonel Hon. George West, 1776-1777
               Lieutenant General Lancelot Baugh, 1777 to war's end

59th Regiment of Foot

COMMANDER: Colonel Gavin Cochrane, 1782 to war's end
LIEUTENANT COLONEL: Robert C. Bayly, to 1777
Gavin Cochrane, 1777-1782
James Dawson, 1783 to war's end
Christopher Horsfall, 1783 to war's end

59th Regiment of Foot   Formed as the 61st Regiment of Foot 1755 and renumbered 1757. Shire designation: 2nd Nottinghamshire. Arrived at Boston 1774, flank companies fighting at Lexington and Concord. As an understrength regiment, men transferred to other regiments while officers returned to England to recruit, 1776. Reformed regiment sent to the relief of Gibraltar October, 1782. Uniform: Officially purple facings, but actually a pinkish crimson, lace with a red and a yellow stripe; officers' metal, gold. Today: The Queen's Lancashire Regiment.

COLONEL: Lieutenant General John Owen, to 1776
Lieutenant General Sir David Lindsay, Bt., 1776 to war's end
LIEUTENANT COLONEL: Otho Hamilton, to 1776
George Grey, 1779 to war's end
Thomas Jones, 1781-1782
William Brown, 1783 to war's end

60th (Royal American) Regiment of Foot   Raised as the 62nd (Royal American) Regiment of Foot 1755 and renumbered 1757. A third and fourth battalion were raised in Hanover and the British Isles, 1775, and of the first two battalions only three weak companies of the 2nd served in North America, the rest serving in the West Indies. The battalions served in the south, fighting at Sudbury and Augusta, Ga., 1779; Port Royal Island, S.C., 1779; Briar Creek, Ga., 1779; the defense of Savannah, 1779; Antigua, 1779; the fall of Baton Rouge; the fall of Mobile and eight companies at the fall of Pensacola. Some 400 men surrendered at St. Vincent June, 1779. Elements sent on invasion of Honduras and Nicaragua and the capture of Fort St. John February, 1780. Survivors of all campaigns sent to St. Augustine, Fla., November, 1782, and then to New York where men were transferred to other regiments while officers were sent to England. Uniform: Blue facings, lace with two blue stripes; officers' metal, silver. Today: 2nd Battalion/The Royal Green Jackets.

COLONEL: General Jeffery Lord Amherst

COMMANDERS: Major General Augustine Prevost, 1775 to war's end

Major General Gabriel Christie, 1777 to war's end

Colonel George Etherington, 1782 to war's end

Colonel Stephen Kemble, 1782 to war's end

LIEUTENANT COLONEL: Augustine Prevost, to 1775

Gabriel Christie, to 1777

George Etherington, to 1782

William Stiell, 1775-1781

Lewis Valentine Fuzer, 1775-1780

Stephen Kemble, 1777-1782

James Mark Prevost, 1781-1782

Beamsley Glazier, 1780 to war's end

William Crosbie, 1780-1783

Archibald MacArthur, 1781 to war's end

Peter Hunter, 1782 to war's end

George Thompson, 1783 to war's end

61st Regiment of Foot   Raised as the 2nd Battalion/3rd Regiment of Foot and designated 61st, 1758. Shire designation: South Gloucestershire. In the garrison of Minorca until its fall February, 1782, returning to England May, 1782 and then sent to Cork December, 1783. Uniform: Buff facings, lace with a blue stripe; officers' metal, gold. Today: The Gloucestershire Regiment.

COLONEL: Colonel John Barlow, to 1778

Lieutenant General Staats Long Morris, 1779 to war's end

COMMANDER: Colonel Charles Gordon, 1783 to war's end

LIEUTENANT COLONEL: George Scott, to 1777

Andrew de la Cour, 1777-1780

John Acklom, 1780-1783

William Gauntlett, 1783 to war's end

62nd Regiment of Foot   Raised as the 2nd Battalion/4th Regiment of Foot 1756 and designated 62nd, 1758. Shire designation: Wiltshire. Arrived for the relief of Quebec May, 1776. Served on the Burgoyne campaign and interned at Saratoga. Uniform: Pale

63rd Regiment of Foot

yellowish buff facings, lace with one yellow stripe between two blue stripes; officers' metal, gold. Today: The Duke of Edinburgh's Royal Regiment.

COLONEL: Lieutenant General William Strode, to 1777
Colonel Valentine Jones, 1777-1780
Major General Edward Mathew, 1780 to war's end
COMMANDER: Colonel John Anstruther, 1780-1782
LIEUTENANT COLONEL: John Anstruther, to 1780
Alexander Campbell, 1782 to war's end

63rd Regiment of Foot　　　Raised 1758. Shire designation: West Suffolk. Arrived at Boston June, 1775, flank companies fighting at Bunker Hill. Sent on the 1776 New York campaign, fighting at Long Island and flank companies at Fort Washington. Sent to Newport November, 1776, returning to New York May, 1777. Sent as reinforcements to Philadelphia, winter, 1777-1778, and returning with the Army to New York, 1778, fighting at Monmouth Court House. Sent to second siege of Charleston December, 1779. Detachments fought at Fishdam Ford, S.C.; Blackstock's Hill, S.C.; Hobkirk's Hill, S.C., and Eutaw Springs, S.C. Sent to the West Indies, where spent the rest of the war, 1782. Uniform: Very dark green facings, lace with a green stripe; officers' metal, gold. Today: The King's Regiment.

COLONEL: Major General Francis Grant, to 1782
Major General Hon. Alexander Leslie, 1782 to war's end
COMMANDER: Major General James Paterson, 1777 to war's end
LIEUTENANT COLONEL: James Paterson, to 1777
Charles Stewart, 1783 to war's end

64th Regiment of Foot　　　Formed 1758. Shire designation: 2nd Staffordshire. Arrived at Boston January, 1769. Sent on the 1776 New York campaign, fighting at Long Island. Sent on the 1777 Philadelphia campaign, fighting at Brandywine and Germantown. Returned with the Army to New York, 1778, fighting at Monmouth Court House. Sent on the Danbury, Conn., raid April, 1777. Sent to the relief of Newport September, 1778, returning to New York and fighting at Old Tappen, N.Y.; capture of Stony Point, N.Y., and Paulus Hook, N.J. Sent to the second siege of Charleston, December, 1779, fighting at Eutaw Springs, S.C. Sent from Charleston to the

West Indies, where it spent the rest of the war, October, 1782. Uniform: Black facings, lace with a black and a red stripe; officers' metal, gold. Today: The Staffordshire Regiment.

COLONEL: Lieutenant General John Pomeroy
COMMANDER: Major General Hon. Alexander Leslie, 1779-1782
LIEUTENANTCOLONEL: Alexander Leslie, to 1775
                      Edmund Eyre, 1782 to war's end

65th Regiment of Foot   Formed 1758. Shire designation: 2nd Yorkshire, North Riding. Arrived at Boston January, 1769, flank companies fighting at Bunker Hill. As an understrength regiment, men transferred to other regiments and officers returned to England to recruit May, 1776. Detachment sent to the relief of Gibraltar as marines on Admiral Lord Howe's fleet, 1782. Regiment sent to Ireland 1783. Uniform: White facings, lace with a mixed red and black stripe and a red stripe; officers' metal, silver. Today: The York and Lancaster Regiment (Disbanded 1968).

COLONEL: Lieutenant General Edward Urmston, to 1779
         Major General Thomas Calcraft, 1779-1783
         Colonel Charles Earl of Harrington, 1783 to war's end
COMMANDER: Colonel Hon. Thomas Bruce, 1779-1782
LIEUTENANT COLONEL: Hon. Thomas Bruce, to 1779
                   Thomas Baskerville, 1782
                   John St. Ledger, 1782 to war's end
                   George Sinclair, 1783 to war's end

An officer's silver swordbelt plate of the 65th Regiment of Foot. (Drawing by Rebecca Katcher)

66th Regiment of Foot   Raised as 2nd Battalion/19th Regiment of Foot 1757 and designated 66th, 1758. Shire designation: Berkshire. Sent from Edinburgh to Ireland fall, 1775, where it spent the war. Uniform: Yellowish green facings, lace with a green stripe between two crimson stripes; officers' metal, gold. Today: The Duke of Edinburgh's Royal Regiment.

COLONEL: Major General Lord Adam Gordon, to 1776

Lieutenant General Joseph Gabbett, 1777 to war's end

COMMANDER: Major General Edward Stopford, 1777 to war's end

LIEUTENANT COLONEL: Edward Stopford, to 1777

67th Regiment of Foot   Formed as the 2nd Battalion/20th Regiment of Foot, 1756, and designated 67th, 1758. Shire designation: South Hampshire. Sent from England and Scotland to Ireland September, 1776, where it served until April, 1785. Uniform: Pale yellow facings, lace with a green, a purple and a yellow stripe in pairs; officers' metal, silver, Today: The Royal Hampshire Regiment.

COLONEL: Lieutenant General Edward Maxwell

LIEUTENANT COLONEL: Hon. Henry St. John, to 1776

James Callander, 1776-1779

Charles Crosbie, 1779-1780

Thomas Pringle, 1780 to war's end

68th Regiment of Foot   Formed as the 2nd Battalion/23rd Regiment of Foot, 1756, and designated 68th, 1758. Shire designation: Durham. Sent from Scotland to Ireland 1775. Due to be sent to Jamaica, but mutinied and was sent instead to Channel Islands, January, 1783. Uniform: Very dark green facings, lace with a black and a yellow stripe; officers' metal, silver. Today: 4th Battalion/The Light Infantry (Disbanded).

COLONEL: General John Lambton

COMMANDER: Colonel Lawrence Reynolds, 1779-1782

LIEUTENANT COLONEL: Lawrence Reynolds, to 1779

Sir Hew Dalrymple, Kt., 1781 to war's end

69th Regiment of Foot   Raised as the 2nd Battalion/24th Regiment of Foot, 1756, and designated 69th, 1758. Shire designation: South Lincolnshire. Served aboard Sir Samuel Hood's fleet, arriving at Barbadoes January, 1781. Sent with the fleet to New York September, 1781, and, although officers tried to have the unit stay in New York with the army, left with Sir Samuel's ships for the West Indies November, 1781. Sent to the relief of St. Kitts, January, 1782, where captured. Uniform: Dull dark green facings, lace with a red stripe between two green ones; officers' metal, gold. Today: The Royal Regiment of Wales.

COLONEL: Lieutenant General Hon. Charles Colvill, to 1776
Lieutenant General Hon. Philip Sherard, 1776 to war's end
COMMANDER: Major General Philip Skene, 1779 to war's end
LIEUTÉNANT COLONEL: Philip Skene, to 1779
William Yorke, 1782 to war's end

70th Regiment of Foot   Formed as the 2/31st Regiment of Foot 1756 and renumbered 1758. Shire designation: Surrey. Arrived from the West Indies at Halifax August, 1778, and spent the entire war there, while flank companies fought in the south. Uniform: Black facings, lace with a black worm; officers' metal, gold. Today: 1st Battalion/The Queen's Regiment.

COLONEL: Lieutenant General Cyrus Trapaud, to 1779
Lieutenant General William Tryon, 1779 to war's end
LIEUTENANT COLONEL: James Bruce, to 1782
Edward Hicks, 1780-1782
Richard St. George, 1782 to war's end

71st Regiment of Foot (Fraser's Highlanders)   Raised in Inverness, Stirling and Glasgow 1775, in two battalions of 2,340 men all told. Arrived at New York July, 1776, fighting at Long Island and Fort Washington. A company on the attack on Forts Clinton and Montgomery. Sent on the 1777 Philadelphia campaign, fighting at Brandywine and Billingsport, N.J., while the 2nd Battalion was sent to Wilmington. Returned to New York December, 1777, fighting at Little Egg Harbour, N.J., October, 1778. A Third Battalion created May, 1777. Grenadier company captured at Stony

Bonnet badge of the 71st Regiment of Foot.

Point July, 1779. Sent to Savannah December, 1778, fighting at Briar Creek, Ga.; Stono Creek, S.C.; the capture of Augusta and the Defense of Savannah. Sent overland to the siege of Charleston December, 1779, fighting at Camden; Charlotte, N.C.; Blackstock's Hill, S.C.; the 1st Battalion at Cowpens, S.C., while the 2nd Battalion at Wetzell's Mills, N.C.; Guilford Court House, N.C.; Green Spring, Va., and interned at Yorktown. The 1st Battalion left Charleston for Halifax November, 1782. Returned to Scotland and disbanded 1783. Uniform: White facings, lace with a red stripe; officers' metal, silver; Highland bonnets and kilts.

COLONEL: Lieutenant General Hon. Simon Fraser

2ND BATTALION COMMANDER: Colonel Alexander Earl of Bal-
carres
LIEUTENANT COLONEL: Hon. John Maitland, to 1779
Alexander McDonald, 1779-1783
Duncan McPherson, 1781-1782
David Ferguson, 1782 to war's end

72nd Regiment of Foot (Royal Manchester Volunteers)   Raised in
Manchester by the city late 1778, and sent to Gibraltar where it
served in the garrison during-the siege. Returned to Manchester and
disbanded 1783. Uniform: White jackets with blue facings.
COLONEL: Colonel Charles Mawhood, to 1781
Major General Charles Ross, 1781 to war's end
COMMANDER: Colonel George Gledstanes, 1782 to war's end
LIEUTENANT COLONEL: George Gledstanes, to 1782

73rd Regiment of Foot (MacLeod's Highlanders)   Two battalions
raised in Scotland 1777. The 2nd Battalion sent to Gibraltar to be
forwarded to Minorca but retained in the Gibraltar garrison during
the siege. The 1st Battalion arrived in India after fighting at the capture of Goree, May, 1779. Flank companies fought in the first battle
of Pollicore. Sent to Madras November, 1780, fighting in the battles
of Porto Novo, July, 1781; Pollicore, August, 1781; Sholinghur,
September, 1781; loss of Trincomalee, August, 1782; defense of
Panianee, November, 1782; defense of Cuddalore, June, 1783; capture of Coondapoor, January, 1783, and the loss of Mangalore,
May-July, 1783. Redesignated 71st Regiment of Foot, 1786. Uni-
form: Green facings; officers' metal, silver; Highland kilts and
bonnets. Today: The Highland Light Infantry.
COLONEL: Major General John Lord MacLeod
2ND BATTALION COMMANDER: Colonel George Mackenzie, 1783
to war's end
LIEUTENANT COLONEL: Duncan McPherson, 1778-1780
George Mackenzie, to 1783
James Craufurd, to 1783
William Dalrymple, 1783 to war's end
John Elphinston, 1783 to war's end

74th Regiment of Foot (Argyll Highlanders) Raised in Scotland December, 1777, and sent to New York, 1779, from where it was sent to Halifax. Sent to Penobscot, Me., for its defense July, 1779. Returned to Scotland and disbanded 1783. Uniform: Yellow facings, lace with a red stripe; officers' metal, gold; Highland kilts and bonnets.

COLONEL: Colonel John Campbell

75th Regiment of Foot (Prince of Wales) Nine companies raised in Wales, 1778, where stationed until disbanded in 1783. It seems likely that some officers from this regiment served in America in other corps. Uniform: Blue facings.

COLONEL: Major General George Morrison, to 1783 (also served as the Army's Quartermaster General)

Colonel Thomas Earl of Lincoln, 1783 to disbanding

76th Regiment of Foot (MacDonell's Highlanders) Raised in the West Highlands and western isles of Scotland, August, 1777, and sent to relief of Jersey Island, then to New York, arriving there August, 1779. Sent to Virginia April, 1781, light company fighting at Petersburg that month, while the whole regiment fought as mounted infantry at Osborne's the same month; Green Spring, Va., and interned at Yorktown. Returned to Scotland and disbanded 1784. Uniform: Deep green facings, lace with a black stripe; officers' metal, gold; Highland kilts and bonnets.

COLONEL: Colonel John MacDonell

LIEUTENANT COLONEL: John Earl of Caithness

Sir Robert Stuart, 1783 to disbanding

77th Regiment of Foot (Athol Highlanders) Raised in Scotland, 1777, for service in Ireland. Due to be sent to America, but men mutinied at Portsmouth and regiment was disbanded there, 1781. Buttons of this regiment have been found in America and it seems as if some of the men were sent to different regiments there.

COLONEL: Colonel John Murray

LIEUTENANT COLONEL: Charles Gordon, to 1783

John Hely Hutchinson, 1783 to disbanding

78th Regiment of Foot (Seaforth Highlanders) Raised in Scotland 1778 and sent to Jersey Island, and then to Bombay May, 1781, where some 450 men became ill within three weeks of landing. Fought at the battle of Arnee, June, 1782; loss of Trincomalee, August, 1782; the defense of Cuddalore, June, 1783, and the capture of Palghautcherry, November, 1783. Redesignated 72nd Regiment of Foot, 1786. Uniform: Yellowish buff facings, bastion lace with a blue stripe; officers' metal, silver. Today: The Queen's Own Highlanders (Seaforth and Camerons).

COLONEL: Lieutenant Colonel Kenneth Earl of Seaforth, to 1782
Lieutenant Colonel T. F. M. Humberston, 1782 to war's end.
LIEUTENANT COLONEL: James Stuart, 1782 to war's end

79th Regiment of Foot (Royal Liverpool Volunteers, Liverpool Blues) Raised in Liverpool by that city January, 1778, with 1,100 men all told. Sent to Jamaica March, 1779, where detachments served as marines. Sent in the invasion of Honduras and Nicaragua and the capture of Fort St. John, February, 1780. Only 84 survivors returned to Liverpool on the ship James and disbanded there February, 1784. Uniform: Blue facings; officers' metal, gold.[7]

COLONEL: Lieutenant General Calcraft, to 1779
Major General Thomas Hall, 1779 to disbanding
LIEUTENANT COLONEL: F. Richmond Humphreys, 1779 to disbanding
Banistre Tarleton, 1781 to disbanding (actually served with the British Legion in America.)

80th Regiment of Foot (Royal Edinburgh Volunteers) Raised in Edinburgh by that city, 1778, and sent to New York August, 1779. History same as the 76th Regiment of Foot (which see.) Uniform: Yellow facings, lace with a red stripe in between two black stripes; officers' metal, silver.

COLONEL: Major General Sir William Erskine, Kt., to 1783
Colonel John Leland, 1783 to disbanding
COMMANDER: Colonel Thomas Dundas, 1782 to disbanding
LIEUTENANT COLONEL: Thomas Dundas, to 1782
James Gordon, 1783 to disbanding

81st Regiment of Foot (Aberdeen Highlanders)

Raised in Aberdeenshire 1778 and served throughout its history in Ireland, returning to Edinburgh and being disbanded in 1783.

COLONEL: Major General Hon. William Gordon
LIEUTENANT COLONEL: Richard Farquhar, to 1783
John Hamilton, 1783 to disbanding

82nd Regiment of Foot

Raised in Lanarkshire 1778 and sent to New York August, 1779. Sent to the defense of Penobscot, Me., July, 1779, and then to Wilmington, N.C., April, 1781. Light company interned at Yorktown. Regiment returned, except for original flank companies which were lost off New Jersey coast to Charleston, then to New York, April, 1782, and then to Halifax, April, 1783, where it was disbanded, 1784. Uniform: Black facings, lace with a black stripe, round hats bound up white; officers' metal, gold.

COLONEL: Colonel Francis MacLean, to 1781
Colonel John Gunning, 1781 to disbanding
LIEUTENANT COLONEL: John Gunning, to 1781
James H. Craig, 1781 to disbanding

83rd Regiment of Foot (Royal Glasgow Volunteers)

Raised in Glasgow by that city 1778 and sent to Jersey Island 1781. From there sent to New York, 1783, being shortly returned to Glasgow and disbanded. Uniform: Blue facings; plain white lace; officers' metal, gold.

COLONEL: Major General George Scott
LIEUTENANT COLONEL: Alexander Fotheringham Ogilvy, to 1781
Henry Fanshawe, 1781
Hon. Malcolm Ramsey, 1781 to disbanding

84th Regiment of Foot (Royal Highland Emigrants)

Raised in Canada from veterans of disbanded Highland regiments and taken onto the regular establishment January, 1779. Sent to the relief of Fort Cumberland November, 1776. The 2nd Battalion sent to Charleston April, 1781, fighting at Eutaw Springs, S.C. Returned to New York April, 1782, and from there to Canada where disbanded

1784. Uniform: Blue facings, lace with one blue stripe in between two red stripes; officers' metal, gold.[8]

    COLONEL: Lieutenant General Sir Henry Clinton, K.B., to 1783

                 Lieutenant General Sir Guy Carleton, K.B., 1783 to disbanding

    1ST BATTALION COMMANDER: Colonel Allan MacLean

    2ND BATTALION COMMANDER: Lieutenant Colonel John Small

85th Regiment of Foot (Westminster Volunteers)   Raised in Westminster by that city July, 1779, and sent to Jamaica, 1780. Returned to Westminster, although many men lost in heavy storms at sea, and survivors disbanded, 1783. Uniform: Bright yellow facings, plain white lace; officers' metal, gold.

    COLONEL: Lieutenant Colonel Charles Lord Harrington, to 1783

                 Lieutenant Colonel Henry Lord Fitzgerald, 1783 to disbanding

86th Regiment of Foot   Raised in England July, 1779, and sent to the Leeward Islands January, 1780. Five companies stationed on Tobago were captured June, 1781. Returned to England and disbanded 1783. Detachments served as marines off America.

    COLONEL: Major General Anthony St. Ledger

    LIEUTENANT COLONEL: Robert Kingston, to 1782

                         Thomas Coore, 1782-1783

                         George Bernard, 1783 to disbanding

87th Regiment of Foot   Raised in England July, 1779, and sent to the Leeward Islands January, 1780. Returned to Coventry, England and disbanded 1783. Uniform: Dark green facings.

    COLONEL: Colonel George Viscount Chewton, to 1780

                 Lieutenant Colonel George Earl of Winchilsea, 1780 to disbanding

88th Regiment of Foot   Raised in England July, 1779, and sent to Jamaica November, 1779. Returned to England, 1781, and disbanded there 1783. Uniform: Bright yellow facings.

    COLONEL: Colonel Thomas Keating

    LIEUTENANT COLONEL: Sir Alexander Leith, Bt., to 1780

Hon. Henry Phipps, 1780-1783
Hon. Charles Gunter Legge, 1783 to disbanding

89th Regiment of Foot   Raised in England July, 1779, and sent to
the Leeward Islands December, 1779. Returned to England and disbanded, 1783. Uniform: Black facings.
   COLONEL: Lieutenant Colonel Hon. Lucius F. Cary, to 1781
                 Major General William Medows, 1781 to disbanding

90th Regiment of Foot (Yorkshire Volunteers)   Raised in
Yorkshire 1775 and sent to the Leeward Islands January, 1780. Re-
turned to Yorkshire and disbanded 1783. Uniform: Officers with
plain cocked hats while other ranks wore white caps and half gaiters.
All ranks wore white wool jackets with scarlet cuffs and collars.
   COLONEL: Major General Lostus A. Tottenham

91st Regiment of Foot (Shropshire Volunteers)   Raised in
Shropshire December, 1779, and sent to St. Lucia and Barbadoes
January, 1780. Many men became ill, much property lost during a
hurricane, and the regiment returned to England June, 1781, where
disbanded 1783.[9] Uniform: Bright yellow facings.
   COLONEL: Colonel Dudley Ackland
   LIEUTENANT COLONEL: Richard Boycott, to 1782
                            William Maxwell, 1782 to disbanding

92nd Regiment of Foot   Raised in England July, 1779, and sent to
Jamaica March, 1780. Returned to England and disbanded 1783.
Uniform: Buff jackets with red cuffs and collars, buff breeches and
trousers, leather caps.
   COLONEL: Lieutenant Colonel Hon. James Stuart

93rd Regiment of Foot   Raised in England July 1779, and sent to
Jamaica February, 1780. Returned to England and disbanded 1783.
Uniform: Officers in red jackets faced yellow; other ranks in blue
jackets with red collars and cuffs.
   COLONEL: Colonel William McCormick

LIEUTENANT COLONEL: James Holwell, 1780-1783
William Keppel, 1783 to disbanding

94th Regiment of Foot   Raised in England July, 1779, and sent to Jamaica February, 1780. Returned to England and disbanded 1783. Uniform: Blue facings.
COLONEL: Colonel James Dundas, to 1781
Major General Robert Prescott, 1781 to disbanding
LIEUTENANT COLONEL: Sir James Murray, Bt., 1780 to disbanding

95th Regiment of Foot   Raised in Yorkshire, 1780, where it served in the defense of Jersey, January 1781. Disbanded in 1783. Uniform: Yellow facings; officers' metal, silver.
COLONEL: Major General John Reid
LIEUTENANT COLONEL: Alexander Campbell

96th Regiment of Foot (British Musketeers)   Raised in England July, 1779, although officers not gazetted until 1780. Sent to Ireland, 1779, and then to the Channel Islands where it was disbanded, 1783. Uniform: Possibly white facings.
COLONEL: Colonel Richard Whyte

97th Regiment of Foot   Raised in England July, 1779, and sent to the relief of Gibraltar March, 1782. Returned to England and disbanded in 1783.
COLONEL: Colonel Samuel Stanton, to 1783
Colonel John Earl of Suffolk, 1783 to disbanding
LIEUTENANT COLONEL: William Macintosh

98th Regiment of Foot   Raised in England 1780 and sent to Bombay May, 1781. Sent on the relief of Cuddalore June, 1783; the capture of Coimbatore, May, 1783, and an expedition against the Polygars of Madura and Tinnelly during the summer of 1783. Returned to England and disbanded, 1785.
COLONEL: Lieutenant Colonel William Fullarton

99th (Jamaica) Regiment of Foot   Raised in Jamaica 1780, where it did garrison duty until disbanded there 1784. Uniform: Light green facings, lace with a red and a green stripe.

100th Regiment of Foot

COLONEL: Major General Charles Rainsford, to 1781
Major General Robert Skene, 1781-1783
Colonel William Gardiner, 1783 to disbanding
LIEUTENANT COLONEL: James Balfour

100th Regiment of Foot   Raised in Ireland 1780 and sent to Bombay May, 1781. Sent to Calcutta, spring, 1782, where it defeated a Mysore army and fought at the defense of Panianee November, 1782. Returned to Ireland and disbanded, 1785.
COLONEL: Colonel Thomas Mackenzie Humberston, to 1782
Major General Hon. Thomas Bruce, 1782 to disbanding
LIEUTENANT COLONEL: John Campbell, 1783 to disbanding

101st Regiment of Foot   Raised in Ireland 1781 and sent to India late 1782. Fought at the defense of Cuddalore, June, 1783, and the siege of Palghaucherry, November, 1783. Returned to Ireland and disbanded, 1785. Uniform: Deep buff facings, lace with a scarlet figure and sky-blue stripe worn in pairs.
COLONEL: Major General Robert Sandford
COMMANDER: Colonel Thomas Adams, 1782 to disbanding
LIEUTENANT COLONEL: Thomas Adams, to 1782
Andrew Gordon, 1781 to disbanding

102nd Regiment of Foot   Raised in Ireland 1781 and had the same history as the 101st Regiment of Foot (which see.) Uniform: Pale buff facings, lace with one yellow and two scarlet stripes.
COLONEL: Major General William Rowley
COMMANDER: Colonel Thomas Jones, 1782 to disbanding
LIEUTENANT COLONEL: Thomas Jones, to 1782
Gordon Forbes, 1781 to disbanding

103rd Regiment of Foot (King's Irish Infantry)   Raised in Ireland 1781, serving there until disbanded, 1783. Uniform: Blue facings.
COLONEL: Colonel Ralph Abercrombie
LIEUTENANT COLONEL: Alexander Ross, 1783 to disbanding

104th Regiment of Foot   Raised in Ireland 1781 where stationed
until disbanded 1783.
   COLONEL: Major General Stuart Douglas
   LIEUTENANT COLONEL: Alexander Leith, 1783 to disbanding
                  Henry Harnage, 1781-1783
                  William Robertson, 1783 to disbanding

105th Regiment of Foot (Volunteers of Ireland)   Raised in
America as the Volunteers of Ireland (which see) of the Provincial
Corps and taken into the Regular establishment April, 1782.
   COLONEL: Colonel Francis Lord Rawdon
   LIEUTENANT COLONEL: Welbore Ellis Duke

TEUCRO DUCE NIL DESPERANDOM.

First Battalion of PENNSYLVANIA LOYALISTS, commanded by His Excellency Sir WILLIAM HOWE, K. B.

ALL INTREPID ABLE-BODIED

HEROES,

WHO are willing to serve His MAJESTY KING GEORGE the Third, in Defence of their Country, Laws and Constitution, against the arbitrary Usurpations of a tyrannical Congress, have now not only an Opportunity of manifesting. their Spirit, by assisting in reducing to Obedience their too-long deluded Countrymen, but also of acquiring the polite Accomplishments of a Soldier, by serving only two Years, or during the present Rebellion in America.

Such spirited Fellows, who are willing to engage, will be rewarded at the End of the War, besides their Laurels, with 50 Acres of Land, where every gallant Hero may retire, and enjoy his Bottle and Lass.

Each Volunteer will receive as a Bounty, FIVE DOLLARS, besides Arms, Cloathing and Accoutrements, and every other Requisite proper to accommodate a Gentleman Soldier, by applying to Lieutenant Colonel ALLEN, or at Captain KEARNY's Rendezvous, at PATRICK TONRY's, three Doors above Market-street, in Second-street.

Provincial Units
in the British Army

BRITISH POLICY ON raising units from among loyal Americans was confused at first. By the war's end, however, a solid, large Provincial Corps had been organized and was doing a large part of the British Army's work in America.

Provincial units may be divided into four types. The first type was the militia, a locally-raised group which was used simply to keep the peace in a British-held area. As these units were not taken into the Provincial Establishment, nor did they serve away from their homes for any time, they are not considered here.

The second type was a Provincial unit copied from the Regular British Army unit. It was trained, armed and uniformed basically the same as Regular British regiments. By December, 1776, uniforms were sent for the Provincial units, consisting of green coats faced white, blue and green. Later, orange, black and buff facings were added. The "regular" Provincial troops were mostly so clad, although it seems as if some regiments, such as the Prince of Wales American Regiment, wore red coats from the start. In the fall of 1777 it was decided that with the start of the 1778 campaign, all Provincial units would be put into red coats with different facings, exactly the same as British regiments.

These Provincial units apparently wore lace of different colors like the British regiments, but the exact design is unknown for any regiment. Many British regiments which, being badly understrength, had their men transferred to other regiments, had their uniforms and supplies sold into Provincial stores, hence it is possible that their lace was used on Provincial coats.

Weapons given Provincial units, too, tended to be the older models of

Provincial Units

Provincial buttons for the Queen's Rangers, left, and Butler's Rangers. The button in the center was a stock pattern issued to most Provincial units which never received a special regimental pattern of their own.

Brown Besses. Delancy's Brigade, for example, first received Brown Besses with wooden ramrods, even though the wooden ramrods had gone out of use many years prior to 1775. The Regiment later passed the old Besses on to the Loyal Queen's County Militia and drew new weapons.

However, the same basic information on the British regiment, officer and private, holds for the "regular" type of Provincial unit.

The third type of Provincial unit was the "ranger" type of unit. With only two regular dragoon regiments sent to America, it was obvious that the Americans would be needed to scout out their rebellious cousins. Such men as Major Robert Rogers had left well-known tales of their ranger work during the French and Indian War, and the Americans would be expected to repeat this type of work.

The ranger type of unit was generally a mixture of men on horse and on foot—the Queen's Rangers had dragoons, huzzars, riflemen, infantrymen and even a kilted Highland company—which was active between the lines. They attacked outposts, skirmished along lines of battle, and patrolled the outskirts of the main army or posts. They were possibly the most effective Provincial units raised, and certainly the most famous.

Early in the war, most ranger units settled on short green or red jackets, trousers and caps like the regular British light infantry caps. Their leather

A typical Provincial ranger wears a hunting shirt, cap, ticking gaiter trousers. He carries a rifle and his hatchet and knife are carried in an old-style British Army waistbelt. (Photograph by Arthur Blundell, courtesy of *Soldier* Magazine.)

accoutrements were often black rather than white. Many of them carried rifles instead of the smoothbore Brown Besses. Their formal structure varied, unlike the "regular" type Provincial units which strictly copied the British Regular regiment.

The last type of Provincial unit was a kind that never actually saw the light of day—or, if actually raised, never reached fulfillment and was either merged into other, larger Provincial units, or simply disbanded. Still, these unit members cannot be classified as militia since they enlisted to serve away from home the same as regular Provincial soldiers. The Berks County Volunteers, a unit of about 40 men raised in Philadelphia and disappearing from sight after the British Army left that city, is an example of that type of unit. Probably the vast majority of men who joined this type of unit were never uniformed and only partly armed or equipped.

Because of problems in recruiting, especially when the Provincial unit was far from home, no hard and fast rules can be stated about the structure of Provincial units in general. An overall figure of each unit's strength is nevertheless given in each unit's listing.

Unlike the Regular British regiment, the man given permission to raise a Provincial regiment often stayed with it and was the colonel in fact as well as title. In some cases, however, the British practice of having a colonel of high rank heading the regiment—at least on paper, but with a lieutenant colonel actually commanding in the field—was followed by some Provincial regiments such as the Pennsylvania Loyalists and the South Carolina Royalists.

PROVINCIAL UNITS

American Legion Raised on Long Island, October, 1780 and stationed there, being sent on raids to Portsmouth, Va., June, 1781, and New London, Conn., September, 1781. Disbanded in Canada, 1783. Strength: 415.

COMMANDER: Brigadier General Benedict Arnold

American Volunteers Major Patrick Ferguson raised this unit after recovering from wounds received leading his first unit of riflemen drawn from British units at Brandywine, in New York, 1779. Unit sent to Charleston, 1780, and participated in back country fighting in the Carolinas, being virtually destroyed at King's Mountain. Strength: 132. Uniform: Green jackets.

Amherst's Corps   Raised in New York and Charleston, 1780, and sent to Jamaica, where it was merged into the Loyal American Rangers or the Duke of Cumberland's Regiment.

COMMANDER: Captain Jeffrey Amherst

Armed Boatmen   Captain William Luce raised about 100 men under this designation.[10]

Black Company of Pioneers   Raised in Philadelphia, late 1777-early 1778, and apparently merged into the Guides and Pioneers in New York, 1778. Each man received a great coat, hat, green sailor's jacket, white shirt and winter trousers. Disbanded in Port Roseway, Canada, 1783. Strength: 90.[11]

COMMANDERS: Captain Allen Stewart

Captain Donald McPherson

British Legion   Raised in New York, July, 1778, from the Caledonian Volunteers (which see) and three other companies. Sent to Savannah, December, 1779 and marched overland to the siege of Charleston. As part of Lord Cornwallis' army, participated in battles in the Carolinas and Virginia. Taken onto the American Establishment as the 5th American Regiment, 7 March, 1781. Interned at Yorktown, while survivors stationed at Charleston and New York were merged into the King's American Dragoons. Unit placed on the British Establishment 25 December, 1782. Strength: 773. Uniform: Green jackets with black facings, white clothes in summer, leather helmets; officers' metal, silver.[12]

COLONEL: Lord William Cathcart

COMMANDER: Lieutenant Colonel Banistre Tarleton

Bucks County Dragoons   Raised in Philadelphia, February, 1778, and participated in raids about the city until returned with the Army to New York, 1778. Attached to the Queen's Rangers (which see) for 1779 campaign; to the British Legion (which see) for 1780 campaign, and permanently merged into that corps in 1782. Strength: 55. Uniforms: Red coats, but ordered into green coats, July, 1778; officers' metal, silver.[13]

Bucks County Volunteers

COMMANDERS: Captain Thomas Stanford, from raising to July, 1778

Captain Christian Huck, from July, 1778, to merger

Bucks County Volunteers   Raised in Philadelphia, early 1778, and served in raids about the city. This infantry unit of about 40 men was commanded by a Captain Thomas and was apparently merged into other Provincial units.[14]

Butler's Rangers   Raised along the New York-Canadian border, December, 1777 and early 1778. In December, 1778, had six companies, growing to ten companies with two light field pieces by 1781. The unit served in border raids in up-state New York and was disbanded in Canada, June, 1784. Uniform: Green jackets, trousers, leather caps; officers' metal, silver.[15]

COMMANDER: Lieutenant Colonel John Butler

Caledonian Volunteers   This partly-mounted, partly-foot company was raised in Philadelphia, late 1777-early 1778, and returned to the Army to New York, 1778. Did outpost duty around New York until merged into the British Legion (which see) July, 1778. Strength: 151 men.[16]

COLONEL: Lord William Cathcart

COMMANDER: Captain William Sutherland

Delancy's Brigade   Raised for the defense of Long Island, September, 1776. The first two battalions were sent to Halifax, then to Savannah, October, 1778, and participated in the taking and later defense of that city. Sent to Charleston, December, 1779, fighting at Eutaw Springs and other actions in the Carolinas. The third battalion remained in the New York garrison. In February, 1782, the first two battalions, which had been combined because of heavy losses into one battalion, were returned to New York, and the entire unit disbanded in New Brunswick, 1783. Strength: first battalion, 584; second battalion, 618, and the third battalion, 550. Uniform: Green coats, later red coats faced blue with buttons arranged evenly, in pairs, or threes depending on the battalion, blanket coats, leather caps and brown wool trousers in the winter; officers' metal, silver.

COMMANDER: Brigadier General Oliver Delancy
FIRST BATTALION COMMANDER: Lieutenant Colonel John Cruger
SECOND BATTALION COMMANDER: Colonel George Brewerton
THIRD BATTALION COMMANDER: Colonel Gabriel Ludlow

Delancy's Refugees (West Chester Refugees)   Raised in New York, fall, 1776, and spent the war serving in raids around that city, being disbanded in Canada, 1783. Uniform: Green coats faced white, brown cloth leggings.[17]

COMMANDER: Major Barmore, from raising to 1777
Lieutenant Colonel James Delancy, 1777 to disbanding

Detroit Volunteer Artillery - see LaMothe's Volunteer Company

Diemar's Huzzars (The Black Huzzars)   Raised of German prisoners taken at Saratoga who escaped to New York, summer, 1778. Served in raids about that city and attached to the Queen's Rangers (which see) 1780. Disbanded and men returned to Germany, 1783. Strength: 80. Uniform: Black or dark gray huzzar jackets.

COMMANDER: Captain Frederich von Diemar

Duke of Cumberland's Regiment   Raised in Charleston, February, 1781, of Continentals captured at Charleston and Camden. Six companies of four officers and 94 men each were sent to Jamaica August, 1781, and spent the war there. A second battalion was raised in 1782 through the merger of the Loyal American Rangers (which see.) Disbanded 24 August, 1783, and the men allowed to settle in Nova Scotia.[18]

COMMANDER: Lord Charles G. Montagu

East Florida Rangers (Florida Rangers, King's Rangers, Carolina Rangers)   Raised along the Georgia-Florida border June, 1779, serving in back country fighting in the south as well as at the defense of Savannah. Merged with the Georgia Loyalists June, 1782. Strength: 860, including some 150 negroes. Uniform: Green, later red, jackets with red facings.

COMMANDER: Lieutenant Colonel Thomas Brown

Emmerich's Chasseurs   Raised in New York, fall, 1776, and stationed there, fighting in the attack on Forts Clinton and Montgomery, and the raid on Tappen, N.Y., September, 1778. Disbanded in Canada 1783. Strength: 250. Uniform, Grey coats or jackets.

COMMANDER: Lieutenant Colonel Andreas Emmerich

First Independent Company of New York Rangers   Raised in New York, fall, 1776, and served there until disbanded. Uniform: Short red coats with blue lapels and cuffs, black hats with a black feather in each.

COMMANDER: Captain Christopher Benson

Georgia Loyalists   Raised in Georgia, 1779, and sent to Charleston December, 1779. Merged with the East Florida Rangers June, 1782, and sent to New York, where disbanded. Strength: 175.

COMMANDER: Major James Wright

Guides & Pioneers   Raised in New York, fall, 1776, and attached to the Loyal American Regiment (which see.) Served at the siege of Newport, 1776-1777, the 1777 Philadelphia campaign, the second siege of Charleston, the attack on Forts Clinton and Montgomery, the 1781 raid into Virginia, and the Danbury, Conn., raid, and disbanded with the Loyal American Regiment. Strength: 250. Uniform: Red jackets with black cuffs and collars.

COMMANDERS: Major Simon Frazer
Major John Aldington

Hierlyhy's Corps   Raised in Nova Scotia, St. Johns and Newfoundland, 1776, and did garrison duty there until sent to New York, July, 1781. Returned to Canada and disbanded, 1783. Strength: 300.

COMMANDER: Major Timothy Hierlyhy

Holland's Pioneers   A red-coated corps of pioneers commanded by a Major Holland which, in the spring of 1777, had at least 50 men stationed in New York.[19]

Independent Companies   Raised in Jamaica, 1780, with one captain, one lieutenant, one ensign, three sergeants, three corporals, two drummers and 40 privates each. Merged into the Loyal American Rangers (which see), 1781.[20]

    FIRST COMPANY COMMANDER: Captain Edward Davis
    SECOND COMPANY COMMANDERS: Captain Park
                                        Captain William Ross Darby

Jamaica Legion   Raised in Jamaica, fall, 1779, and sent on the invasion of Honduras and Nicaragua, participating in the capture of Fort St. John, February, 1780. Merged into the Jamaica Volunteers (which see) October, 1780. Strength: 213 men in four companies.[21]

    COMMANDER: Major John Dalrymple

Jamaica Rangers   A negro corps raised in the summer of 1779, each battalion to consist of one major, commanding; six captains; one captain-lieutenant; seven lieutenants; eight ensigns; one chaplain; one adjutant; one quartermaster; one surgeon and two mates; 24 sergeants; 24 corporals; 16 drummers, and 376 privates. A third battalion was authorized 19 October, 1782. The ultimate disposition of this unit is unknown. Uniform: White coats faced red.[22]

    FIRST BATTALION COMMANDER: Major William Henry Ricketts
    SECOND BATTALION COMMANDER: Major William Lewis
    THIRD BATTALION COMMANDER: Major Nathaniel Beckford

Jamaica Volunteers   Raised in the fall of 1779 and having the same history as the Jamaica Legion (which see.) Reinforced through the merger of the Jamaica Legion and the Royal Batteaux men February, 1780. Disbanded in Jamaica April, 1781. Strength: 258 men in five companies.[23]

    COMMANDER: Major John Macdonald

James' Troop of Provincial Dragoons   Raised in Chester County, Pa., January-February, 1778, and participated in raids around Philadelphia. Served with, and similar history to, the Bucks County Dragoons (which see.) Uniform: Green coats ordered July, 1778.[24]
COMMANDER: Captain Jacob James

Jessup's Corps   Raised in Canada, 1775, and sent on Burgoyne campaign, being virtually destroyed at Bennington, Vt. Uniform: Red coats faced green.[25]
COMMANDER: Major Ebenezer Jessup

Johnson's Royal Greens (Johnson's Royal Regiment of New York, King's Royal Regiment of New York)   Raised in Tyron County, N.Y., 1776, fighting at Oriskany, August, 1777; the raid on the Wyoming Valley; battle of Klock's Field, October, 1780, and Jerseyfield, October, 1781. Detachments served at siege of Fort Stanwix, August, 1777, and siege of Fort Schuyler, 1777. A second battalion created 1780. Disbanded in Canada June, 1784. Strength: 1,290. Uniform: Green coats faced blue, white or red, later red coats faced blue.
COMMANDER: Colonel Sir John Johnson

King's American Dragoons   Raised in New York February, 1781, from several independent mounted companies and spent the rest of the war there until disbanded in Halifax April, 1783. Strength: 350. Uniform: Red coats faced blue, dragoons' helmets; officers' metal, gold.[26]
COMMANDER: Lieutenant Colonel Benjamin Thompson

King's American Regiment   Raised in New York December, 1776 as the Associated Refugees. Spent 1777 in New York, serving at Forts Clinton and Montgomery, then sent to the relief of Newport, July, 1778. Returned to New York, June, 1779, and sent on raids into Virginia, 1780, being then sent to Charleston, then to Savannah. Took part in operations in Georgia and East Florida, with a detachment at King's Mountain. The unit was taken on by the American Establishment as the 4th American Regiment, 7 March, 1781. Taken on by the British Establishment on 25 December, 1782, possibly as the 110th Regiment of Foot. Disbanded in Canada, 1783.

A private of Johnson's Royal Greens. His gaiters were made by cutting down the full gaiters, such as worn by German troops, to knee-length. He wears a brass engraved waistbelt plate. (Drawing by George C. Woodbridge, courtesy of the *Brigade Dispatch*.

King's Orange Rangers

Strength: 833. Uniform: Red coats faced blue; officers' metal, gold.

COLONEL: Colonel Edmund Fanning

COMMANDER: Lieutenant Colonel George Campbell

King's Orange Rangers   Raised as a mounted rifle company, Orange County, N.Y., December, 1776. One company served at Fort Montgomery before the unit was sent to Halifax, October, 1778. Disbanded there, 1783. A detachment served in the 1779-1780 Charleston campaign with the Volunteers of Ireland. Strength: 600. Uniform: Green coats, later red coats faced orange; officers' metal, silver.

COMMANDERS: Captain John Coffin
Lieutenant Colonel John Bayard

King's Rangers   After Lieutenant Colonel Robert Rogers gave up command of the Queen's Rangers, he left for Nova Scotia where he raised this unit of about 250 men in 1777. It served throughout the war there, being disbanded in 1783.

LaMothe's Volunteer Company   Raised in the northwestern territories in the spring of 1778, it was stationed at Poste Vincennes, serving at several expeditions into enemy held territories. Strength: 45.[27]

COMMANDER: Captain LaMothe

Loyal American Association   Raised in Boston, April, 1775, and served at the siege there. Left with main army, serving at Long Island and around New York, 1776, when, as an understrength unit, men transferred to other Provincial units. Uniform: Civilian clothes with a white sash worn on the left arm.[28]

COMMANDER: Brigadier General Timothy Ruggles

Loyal American Rangers   Raised in New York 1780, from Continental prisoners and deserters, about 300 men in six companies, each with three officers, three sergeants, four corporals and 67 privates. Sent to Kingston, Jamaica, February, 1781, and then on to Pensacola, but returned before arriving there on receiving word of that city's fall. Eighty men sent on the raid on Black River, Honduras, August, 1782. On the commander's death, 6 January, 1783, the unit merged with the Duke of Cumberland's Regiment (which see.)[29]

COMMANDER: Major William Odell

Loyal American Regiment   Raised in New York, fall, 1776, and elements took part in the 1777 Philadelphia campaign. Took part in attacks on Forts Clinton and Montgomery, and the raid on Portsmouth, Va., returning to New York June, 1781. Sent on the New London, Conn., raid, August, 1781. Sent to Nova Scotia and disbanded 1783. Strength: 693: Uniform: Green coats, later red coats faced buff and/or green; officers' metal, gold.

COMMANDER: Colonel Beverly Robinson

Loyal Foresters   Raised in New York, 1781, and sent to Virginia April, 1781, to recruit more, where the commander was captured. Men interned at Yorktown. Strength: 80.[30]

COMMANDER: Lieutenant Colonel John Connolly

Loyal Irish Volunteers   Captain James Forrest raised this unit in Boston April, 1775, and they were merged into the Loyal American Association (which see.) Uniform: A white cockade.[31]

Loyal New Englanders   Permission granted for raising this unit 21 March, 1777, and recruiting began in Newport, R.I., that year. It was to consist of ten companies with 32 officers, 30 sergeants, 30 corporals, 10 drummers and 500 privates, but it actually reached a top strength of only about 82 men.[32] It was merged, as an understrength regiment, into other Provincial regiments, August, 1779.[33]

COMMANDER: Lieutenant Colonel George Wrightman

Loyal Newport Associators   Three companies, of 180 men, raised in Newport, October, 1777, for service in the siege of that city.

COMMANDER: Colonel Wanton

Loyal Nova Scotia Volunteers (Royal Nova Scotia Volunteers) Raised in Nova Scotia December, 1775, and stationed there until disbanded, October, 1783. Unit was granted the "Royal" designation after 1780. Strength: 775. Uniform: Green coats faced white, later red coats faced green and/or buff; officers' metal, gold.[34]

COMMANDERS: Governor Francis Legge, from raising to 1782
Colonel John Parr, 1782 to disbanding

Loyal Refugees Formed in New York, 1778, and sent later that year to East Florida where it made raids into Georgia until disbanded in St. Augustine, 1783.

COMMANDER: Moses Kirkland

Maryland Loyalists Formed in Philadelphia, fall, 1777, and returned with the Army to New York, 1778. Sent to Halifax September, 1778, and on to Jamaica, December, 1778. From Jamaica to Pensacola, January, 1779, where it served until that post fell, May, 1781. As prisoners sent to Havana, Cuba, for one month, and then paroled to New York. Exchanged for Spanish prisoners July, 1782, and spent the rest of the war in garrison duty in New York until sent to New Brunswick where disbanded, 1783. Strength: 425. Uniform: Red coats faced olive green; officers' metal, silver.[35]

COMMANDER: Lieutenant Colonel James Chalmers

Nassau Blues Raised in New York May, 1779, and disbanded that December. Strength: 60

COMMANDER: Colonel William Axtell

The Negro Horse Raised in New York 1782 to patrol outside lines and pick up deserters, fighting in a skirmish at Dorchester April, 1782. Strength: 100.

COMMANDER: (?)

Newfoundland Regiment Raised in Newfoundland September, 1780, and stationed there until disbanded, 1783. Placed on the British Establishment 25 December, 1782. Uniform: Blue coats faced red, plain white lace worn in pairs.[36]

COMMANDER: Major Robert Pringle

New Jersey Volunteers (Skinner's Greens)   Initially three battalions raised in New York, 1776, although eventually six battalions fielded. The battalions served in the New York garrison until one battalion sent to East Florida and then to the capture of Savannah, fighting at that city's defense, Eutaw Springs, King's Mountain, and a detachment at Yorktown. The third battalion sent on New London, Conn., raid, August, 1781. All battalions disbanded in New Brunswick, 1783. Strength: first battalion, 887; second battalion, 718; third battalion, 845. Uniform: Green coats, later red coats faced blue; officers' metal, silver.

REGIMENTAL COMMANDER: Brigadier General Cortland Skinner
FIRST BATTALION COMMANDER: Lieutenant Colonel Joseph
                                    Barton
SECOND BATTALION COMMANDER: Lieutenant Colonel John
                                    Morris
THIRD BATTALION COMMANDER: Lieutenant Colonel Issac Allen
FOURTH BATTALION COMMANDER: Lieutenant Colonel Abraham
                                    Van Buskirk

New York Volunteer Rifle Company   Raised in New York, fall, 1776, originally as part of Emmerich's Chasseurs, then transferred to the New York Volunteers (which see.) The company served with the Queen's Rangers (which see) in Virginia, 1781. Uniform: Green jackets.

COMMANDER: Captain John Althaus

New York Volunteers   Raised in Halifax January-February, 1776, and two companies sent on New York 1776 campaign. Unit at the raid on Forts Clinton and Montgomery. Sent to East Florida, October, 1778, and present at the defense of Savannah, September, 1779; siege of Charleston, April, 1780, and the Battles of Camden and Hobkirk's Hill. Returned to Savannah and sent back to New York, August, 1782. Disbanded in Canada, 1783. Placed on the American Establishment as the 3rd American Regiment 2 May, 1779.

A company officer of the 2nd Battalion, the New Jersey Volunteers. (Drawing by Dennis Martin, courtesy of the *Brigade Dispatch.*)

Strength: 475. Uniform: Green coats, later red coats faced buff and/or blue; officers' metal, gold.

COMMANDERS: Captain Archibald Campbell, from raising to March, 1777

Major Alexander Grant, March, 1777-October, 1777

Lieutenant Colonel George Turnbull, October, 1777 to disbanding

North Carolina Highlanders (North Carolina Volunteers)   Raised in North Carolina, 1780, serving in the Carolinas until sent to New York, 1782, and disbanded in Canada, 1783. Strength: 611. Uniform: Blue jackets, government sett kilts from the stores of the 71st Regiment of Foot.

COLONEL: Governor Joseph Martin

COMMANDER: Lieutenant Colonel Samuel Bryan

Pennsylvania Loyalists   Raised in Philadelphia, September, 1777, and had the same history as the Maryland Loyalists (which see). Strength: 200. Uniform: Red coats faced olive green, trousers; officers' metal, gold.[37]

COLONEL: Sir William Howe

COMMANDER: Lieutenant Colonel William Allen

Philadelphia Light Dragoons   Raised in Philadelphia, November, 1777, and attached to various units such as the Queen's Rangers and British Legion until merged into the King's American Dragoons (which see,) 1782. Strength: 121. Uniform: Green coats.

COMMANDER: Captain Richard Hoveden

Prince of Wales American Regiment   Raised in New York, largely of Connecticut men, early 1777, and sent to the relief of Newport, June, 1778. Returned to New York 1779, and sent to the Bahamas, then to Charleston April, 1779. Fought at Hanging Rock, S.C., where commanded by Major Carden. Returned to New York June, 1783, and disbanded later that year in Canada. Strength: 610. Uniform: Red coats faced blue and/or green; officers' metal, gold.

COMMANDER: Brigadier General Monteforte Brown

In the field—the typical Provincial.
A private of the Pennsylvania Loyalists, with his regimental lace removed for field use. His cartridge box is a pattern gone out of use by Regular types, and he wears his waistbelt over his shoulder. (Drawing by George C. Woodbridge, courtesy of the *Brigade Dispatch*.)

While a private of the Prince of Wales American Regiment places his Brown Bess in a bell of arms tent, used for arms storage, a light company man and a battalion officer talk. The private in the background wears typical fatigue wear. (Drawing by Dennis Martin, courtesy of The Company of Military Historians.)

Provincial Light Dragoons

Provincial Light Dragoons (Stewart's Troop of Guides and Expresses, The Staten Island Troop of Light Horse)   Raised on Staten Island, N.Y., 1779, and took part in raids into New Jersey. Merged into the King's American Dragoons (which see,) February, 1782. Uniform: Red coats faced blue, dragoons helmets.[38]

COMMANDER: Captain William Stewart

Provincial Light Battalion   As in the British Army, the flank companies of Provincial units were brigaded together. The battalion in the north was commanded by Lieutenant Colonel John Watson, while the southern battalion, which had 194 men in September, 1780, was commanded by Major Thomas Barclay. The men wore their regular regimental uniforms.

Queen's Loyal Rangers   Raised in Canada, where stationed until disbanded in 1783, from survivors of the Burgoyne campaign. Uniform: Green coats.[39]

COMMANDER: Major Ebenezer Jessup

Queen's Loyal Virginia Regiment   Raised in Virginia November, 1775, and fought at Great Bridge, Va. After the commander's capture, early 1776, the unit was sent to New York and merged into the Queen's Rangers (which see.) Strength: 600.

COMMANDER: Lieutenant Colonel John Ellegood

Queen's Rangers   Raised in New York and western Connecticut and with men from the Queen's Loyal Virginia Regiment August, 1776. Sent with the Army on 1777 Philadelphia campaign, fighting at Brandywine and Germantown. Returned with the Army to New York, 1778, fighting at Monmouth Court House. Taken on the American Establishment as the 1st American Regiment, 2 May, 1779. Sent to Virginia, 1781, and interned at Yorktown. Parts of the unit stationed in New York merged into the King's American Dragoons. Taken on the British Establishment 25 December, 1782. Strength: 937. Uniform: Green jackets with dark blue or black facings, black leather accoutrements, a huzzar company in that dress, and a highland company, complete with piper, in government sett kilts. Today: The Queen's York Rangers.[40]

COMMANDERS: Colonel Robert Rogers, from raising to May, 1777

Lieutenant Colonel Christopher French, May, 1777 to August, 1777

Major James Wemys, August, 1777-October, 1777

Lieutenant Colonel John Simcoe, October, 1777 to disbanding.

Roman Catholic Volunteers   Raised in Philadelphia, October, 1777, from loyal Irish. Sent with Army to New York, 1778, but discipline fell apart and the unit was merged into the Volunteers of Ireland 25 October, 1778. Strength: 14 officers and 212 other ranks in four companies.[41]

COMMANDER: Lieutenant Colonel Alfred Clifton

Royal American Reformees   Raised in New York, 1777 from deserters from the Continental Army and stationed there until disbanded, in Canada, 1783. Strength: 120.

COMMANDER: Lieutenant Colonel Rudolph Ritzema

Royal Batteaux Men   Raised in Jamaica, fall, 1779 and had the same history as the Jamaica Volunteers (which see.) Strength: 125.[42]

COMMANDER: Lieutenant Colonel Alexander Leith, BT.

Royal Fencible Americans   Raised in Nova Scotia, June, 1775, of Europeans and Continental rifle battalion deserters. Stationed in Nova Scotia until disbanded, 1783. Strength: 462. Uniform: Green coats faced white, later red coats faced blue, black and/or buff; officers' metal, silver.[43]

COMMANDER: Lieutenant Colonel Joseph Gorham

Royal Garrison Regiment (Royal Bermudian Regiment)   Raised in New York, September-October, 1778 of men unable to perform active duties in regular regiments. The unit's one battle was the defense of Paulus Hook, N.J., 18-19 August, 1779. Two companies sent to Bermuda, fall, 1778, and a detachment to Halifax, late 1778-early 1779. Two companies captured by Spanish 8 May 1782 and paroled to England. Unit placed on British Establishment 25 December 1782 and disbanded in 1784, with the men allowed to go to England, rather than Canada because of the effects of the harsh winters on the men's poor health. Strength: 800. Uniform: Red coats with blue and/or green facings.[44]

COMMANDERS: Major William Sutherland from raising to 24 October 1779

Lieutenant Colonel Robert Donkin, 24 October 1779 to disbanding

Royal Highland Emigrants   Raised in Nova Scotia and placed on the British Establishment as the 84th Regiment of Foot (which see), January, 1779.

Royal Honourable Americans   Raised in Boston, 1775, and served as part of the Loyal American Association (which see).[45]

COMMANDER: Lieutenant Colonel Joseph Gorham

Royal North Carolina Regiment   Raised in Charleston, S.C., spring, 1780, serving there, Camden, S.C., and the Battle of Hanging Rock, S.C. Sent to St. Augustine, Fla., November, 1782, and disbanded there, 1783. Strength: 600. Uniform: Red coats faced blue; buttonholes in pairs; officers' metal, gold.

COMMANDER: Lieutenant Colonel John Hamilton

St. Johns Volunteers   Raised in Nova Scotia, February, 1777, and stationed there until disbanded, 1783. Strength: 43.

COMMANDER: Captain Phillips Callbeck

South Carolina Dragoons   Raised in Charleston, January, 1781, and served with the South Carolina Royalists (which see.) Strength: 38.

COMMANDER: Captain Edward Fenwick

South Carolina Rangers   Raised in Charleston, June, 1780, where it served until sent to St. Augustine, Fla., November, 1782, and disbanded there, 1783. Strength: 81.

COMMANDER: Major John Harrison

South Carolina Royalists   Raised in East Florida, May, 1778, in two troops of rifle dragoons and four companies of infantry. Sent to Savannah, August, 1779, and on to Charleston, May, 1780. Served at Ninety-Six and Hobkirk's Hill. Converted to cavalry, June, 1781, and sent from Charleston to the relief of Ninety-Six. Fought at Eutaw Springs and Waldboo Plantation, August, 1782. Sent to New York, November, 1782, and disbanded there. Strength: 660. Uniform: Red coats faced yellow.

    COLONEL: Alexander Innes
    COMMANDERS: Major M. Prevost, while in Georgia
                 Major John Coffin, 1780-1782
                 Major Thomas Frasor, for last battles

Starkloff's Troop of Light Dragoons   Raised in Charleston, April, 1781, by taking 60 men from each of the Hessian Regiments von Türmbach, von Bose and Prinz Carl. Uniform: Green jackets.[46]

    COMMANDER: Captain Frederich Starckloff

Volunteers of Ireland   Raised in Philadelphia, fall, 1777, and returned to New York with the Army, 1778. Sent to Charleston, December, 1779, fighting in actions in the Carolinas. Placed on the American Establishment as the 2nd American Regiment, 2 May, 1779, and on the British Establishment as the 105th Regiment of Foot, 25 December, 1782. Departed for England April, 1783, and disbanded there. Strength: 871. Uniform: Red coats without lapels but with green brandenbergs.

    COMMANDER: Colonel Francis Lord Rawdon

Volunteers of New England   Raised in New York, spring, 1781, and merged into the King's American Dragoons, February, 1782. Strength: 33.

    COMMANDER: Major Joshua Upham

Wentworth's Volunteers   Raised in Boston, summer, 1775, and went with the Army on 1776 New York campaign. As an understrength regiment, merged into other Provincial regiments. Strength: 43. Uniform: Red coats.

    COMMANDER: Major Daniel Murray

West Florida Loyalists

West Florida Loyalists   Raised in West Florida, 1779, serving at the fall of Pensacola May, 1781. They were not sent to Havana with the rest of the prisoners, and seem to have disbanded themselves after the city's fall. Strength: 75.
COMMANDER: (?)

West Florida Royal Foresters   Raised in West Florida 1780 and disbanded after the fall of Pensacola May, 1781. Strength: 43.
COMMANDER: Captain Adam Chrystie

West Jersey Cavalry   Raised in Philadelphia May, 1778, and sent to New York with the Army, 1778, where they were stationed until merged into the King's American Dragoons (which see,) February, 1781. Strength: 160. Uniform: Red coats.
COMMANDER: Lieutenant Colonel John Van Dyke

West Jersey Volunteers   Raised in Philadelphia, January, 1778, and sent to New York with the Army, 1778, where they were merged into the New Jersey Volunteers (which see.) Strength: 200. Uniform: Red coats.
COMMANDER: Major John Van Dyke, until 1778
Lieutenant Colonel David Coxe, 1778 until merger

German Units
in the British Employ

WHEN HOSTILITIES BROKE out in America in 1775 the British government turned to the source of troops it had relied on in many wars and rebellions of the times, the various German states. German troops had been used by the British government against its own rebellious subjects during the Jacobite uprising of 1745 in Scotland.

In addition, King George was also ruler of the German state of Hanover, and regiments from Hanover were already in his service. By the war's end, two Hanovarian regiments had fallen in Minorca; two more were fighting in India, and three more served in the Gibraltar garrison during the siege.

Treaties were drawn up with the rulers of Hesse Cassel, Hesse Hanau, Brunswick, Waldeck, Anspach-Beyreuth and Anhalt Zerbst for their troops to be used in America. Hesse Cassel was to supply 19 regiments of foot, an artillery corps, jaegers and supporting troops; Brunswick, five regiments of foot, one grenadier battalion, supporting artillery and a dragoon regiment; Anspach-Beyreuth, two foot regiments, an artillery company and jaegers, and Hesse Hanau, Waldeck and Anhalt Zerbst, one foot regiment and supporting artillery, each. Each unit is listed with its country of origin.

The basic German regiment was made up of one battalion with one grenadier company, although the Brunswick and Hesse Hanau regiments had light companies as well. An infantry battalion was supposed to have 21 officers, five non-combatant officers (chaplain, surgeon, etc.), 60 sergeants and corporals, 22 drummers and 525 privates. As was common on all sides, regiments were usually understrength.

Philip Cavanaugh, a grenadier of the re-created Fusilier Regiment von Ditfurth, wears his regiment's authentically reconstructed uniform. The regiment's grenadiers wore tall, pewter fronted caps with yellow bags in the cap part. Their blue coats are lined with red with yellow cuffs and lapels and have white worsted tape binding. Sleeves on German coats were cut short to make the soldiers appear taller. Small clothes are white, with tall black gaiters. He wears a waistbelt with short sword and bayonet and his musket has a red leather sling. Unlike most 18th century men, German grenadiers wore moustaches.

From behind, one can see the metal canteen, calfskin covered knapsack and heavy cartridge box worn by German troops. The building in the background is the barracks at Trenton, N.J., where Hessian troops were stationed that unfortunate night of December 25, 1776. Note the yellow shoulder strap used to hold the box sling in place.

To conform to British practices, the grenadier companies were taken from the battalions and regimented together.

As was typical with British regiments, the German regimental colonel, or "chief," rarely served with his regiment. There was a commander appointed who, often, was a person of higher rank than might actually command a regiment. In that case a field commander would be appointed. In some units, particularly the newer ones, two or even all three ranks may be held by one man. Generally, the regiment took the chief's name for its designation.

The typical musketeer, or private, wore a black hat with white binding and a colored pompon in it. His waistcoat and breeches were either light yellow or white, depending on the regiment. He wore a long pair of black linen gaiters over his breeches, stockings and shoe tops.

Unlike the British, who were by now mostly wearing their bayonet belts over their shoulders, the Germans wore theirs around their waists. They also all carried short swords, although all British troops except grenadiers and sergeants had laid theirs aside by this period.

The German coat was of blue wool, often collarless, with short lapels (garrison regiments did not wear lapels), cuffs, and a shoulder strap on the left shoulder of a facing color. The coat was usually lined red, and the buttons were of plain pewter or brass.

The cartridge box was a large, heavy affair, usually decorated with a large plate bearing his prince's coat-of-arms. Across the other shoulde he slung a knapsack of hairy animal hide. His tin canteen was the same as the British model.

The typical German musket was a copy of the Prussian musket. It was much like the British Brown Bess, being pin-fastened with brass furniture and .75 calibre in size.

German sergeants had their uniforms laced in silver, usually, and carried a halberd, or long pole with an elaborate blade on the end. Officers wore still finer and more decorated uniforms and carried spontoons. Many of them preferred boots to shoes and gaiters, and many wore large gorgets under their coats. Their sashes were wide and made of different colors according to their individual states.

A unique German organization was the corps of jaegers, or hunters. These were originally raised from among hunters and game wardens of the German forests, and they were armed with heavy, short rifles, instead of muskets. Although in detail they slightly differed from state to state, jaegers generally wore green coats with red facings and linings, and large cocked hats. They were especially hired by the British government because it was thought they would be at an advantage in the vast American forests. As it turned out, however, many plain peasants were put into

The Hessian cartridge box bears plates made as flaming grenades in each corner and a large center plate with the lion of Hesse Kassel and Prinz Frederich's cypher. (Reconstructions made by the Grenadier Company, Fusilier Regiment von Ditfurth.)

jaeger uniform, rather than the especially-trained hunters, and the jaeger units were little better, at times, than regular battalion soldiers.

Many contemporaries referred to German units by English or French translations of their actual name. Thus, for example, the Lieb Infantry Regiment became, to them, Regiment Du Corps, or German Guards. In this list the German designations have been used.

GERMAN UNITS

The Anhalt Zerbst Regiment (Frie Corps)   Arrived at Quebec, May, 1778, and sent to New York, August, 1781, spending the war there until returned to Germany, 1783. Strength: 11 officers, 463 other ranks in two battalions. Uniform: White coats, faced red, felt caps, boots, red cloaks, red and yellow worsted sashes worn by all ranks.[47]

> COMMANDER: Colonel Baron von Rauchenplatt
> FIRST BATTALION COMMANDER: Major von Piquet
> SECOND BATTALION COMMANDER: Colonel von Rauchenplatt

1st Regiment Anspach-Beyreuth 1777-1779: **Regiment von Voit,** 1779-1783: **1st Anspach Battalion,** 1783   Arrived New York, June, 1777. Sent to Philadelphia November, 1777, and returned to New York with the Army, 1778. Sent to the relief of Newport, July, 1778, and returned to New York, October, 1779. Sent to Virginia, May, 1781, and interned at Yorktown. Returned to Germany, May, 1783. Strength: 27 officers, 543 other ranks. Uniform: Red facings, white small clothes.

> COMMANDERS: Colonel F.L.A. von Eby, to May, 1778
> Colonel F.A.V. Voit von Salzburg, May, 1778
> through war's end

2nd Regiment Anspach-Beyreuth, 1777-1779: **Regiment Seybothen,** 1779-1782: **2nd Anspach Battalion,** 1783   Regimental history and strength same as 1st Regiment Anspach-Beyreuth (which see.) Uniform: Black facings, white small clothes.

> COMMANDERS: Colonel F.A.V. Voit von Salzburg, to May, 1778
> Colonel F.J.H.W.C. von Seybothen, May, 1778 to
> war's end

Anspach Artillery   Arrived with the Anspach infantry regiments and served with them. Strength: two field guns, one officer, 43 other ranks. Uniform: Red facings, yellow buttons, white small clothes.
COMMANDER: Captain N. F. Hofmann

Hesse Hanau Artillery Company   Arrived with the Hesse Hanau Regiment (which see) and had the same history. Uniform: Crimson facings, yellow small clothes.
COMMANDER: Captain Georg Pausch

Artillery Corps of Hesse Cassel   Served in detachments with all the various infantry regiments of Hesse Cassel throughout the war. Strength at New York, October, 1778: 373 men. Uniform: Red facings.
CHIEF: Lieutenant General J.J. von Gohr
COMMANDER: Major H. Heitel

Light Infantry Battalion von Barner (Brunswick)   Participated in the Burgoyne campaign and interned at Saratoga. Made up of the light companies of different Brunswick regiments and the Brunswick jaeger company. Strength: 24 officers, 634 other ranks.[48]
COMMANDER: Lieutenant Colonel F.A. von Barner

Regiment von Barner (Brunswick)   Created in 1778 from survivors of the Saratoga campaign and new European recruits. The battalion did garrison duty in Canada until returned to Germany, 1783.[49]
COMMANDER: Lieutenant Colonel F.A. von Barner

Garrison Regiment von Benning   (see Garrison Regiment von Huyn)

2nd Battalion Grenadiere von Block, 1776-1777; **2nd Battalion Grenadiere von Lengerke**, 1777-1783 (Hesse Cassel)   Arrived in New York, August, 1776. Made up of grenadier companies of various Hesse Cassel infantry regiments. Sent to Philadelphia, 1777, fighting at Red Bank, N.J. Returned to New York with the Army, 1778, and sent to Charleston, December, 1779. Returned to New York, November, 1782, and on to Germany, 1783.

COMMANDER: Lieutenant Colonel von Block, to 1777
Lieutenant Colonel von Lengerke, 1777 to war's end

Musketeer Regiment von Bose (see Musketeer Regiment von Türmbach)

Grenadiere Battalion von Breymann (Brunswick) Arrived at Quebec, June, 1776. Made up of grenadier companies of Brunswick regiments. Served in the Burgoyne campaign and interned at Saratoga. Strength: 19 officers, 545 other ranks. Uniform: Various uniforms according to the men's regiments.[50]

COMMANDER: Lieutenant Colonel H.C. Breymann, to October, 1777
Lieutenant Colonel O.C.A. von Mengen, October, 1777, to war's end

Garrison Regiment von Bünau (Hesse Cassel) Arrived at New York, October, 1776. Sent to the relief of Newport, November, 1776. Returned to New York on abandonment of that post and sent back to Germany, 1783. Strength, August, 1778: 16 officers, 508 other ranks. Uniform: Scarlet collar and cuffs, changed in 1783 to crimson collar and cuffs, no lapels, white small clothes; officers' lace, silver.

COMMANDER: Colonel R. von Bünau

Chasseurs (Hesse Cassel) Drawn from Regiments Landgraf, von Ditfurth, von Huyn, and von Bunau, September, 1777, at Newport, two companies of four officers and 150 other ranks. First company commander: Captain F.W. von der Malsburg, Regiment von Ditfurth. Second company commander: Captain-Lieutenant A.C. Noltenius, Regiment von Bünau. Companies disbanded 25 November, 1778, and men returned to their regiments. New chasseur company raised 21 July, 1778, at New York by taking two men each from the Regiments Lieb, Erbprinz, Prinz Carl, Donop, Mirbach, Türmbach,

Lossberg (alt), Knyphausen, Wöllwarth and Seitz, for a total of four officers and 115 other ranks. Commander: Captain-Lieutenant George Hanger. Disbanded and men returned to their regiments 15 November, 1778. Hanger raised a new chasseur company 10 December, 1779, which was sent to Charleston. The company returned to New York and was disbanded, December, 1780. The men wore their regular regimental uniforms.[51]

Grenadiere Regiment d'Angelelli   (see Grenadiere Regiment von Rall)

Fusilier Regiment von Ditfurth (Hesse Cassel)   Arrived at New York, August, 1776, fighting at Fort Washington and White Plains. Sent to Newport, November, 1776, and returned to New York, 1779. Sent to Charleston, December, 1779, serving in the garrison there until returned to New York, November, 1782. Returned to Germany, November, 1783. Redesignated a musketeer regiment, 1782. Strength, August, 1778: 17 officers, 532 other ranks. Uniform: Bright yellow facings, white lace which was removed when they became musketeers, white small clothes; officers' lace, silver.
    CHIEF: Lieutenant General W.M. von Ditfurth
    COMMANDER: Colonel C. von Bose, to 1777
                     Colonel M. von Westerhagen, 1777 to war's end

Musketeer Regiment von Donop (Hesse Cassel)   Arrived in New York, August, 1776, fighting at Fort Washington and in the 1777 New Jersey campaign. Sent on the 1777 Philadelphia campaign, fighting at Brandywine and Germantown. Returned with the Army to New York, 1778, and stationed there until returned to Germany, November, 1783. Strength, October, 1778: 458 men. Uniform: Pale yellow facings, yellow small clothes, red stocks; officers' lace, gold.
    CHIEF: Lieutenant General H.A. von Donop
    COMMANDER: Colonel D.U. von Gosen, to 1780
                     Colonel C.P. Heymell, 1780 to war's end

Regiment von Ehrenkrook (Brunswick)   Created from survivors of the Saratoga campaign, 1778, spending the rest of the war in garri-

A field officer of the Fusilier Regiment von Ditfurth rides by, from left, a fusilier and a grenadier of the Regiment. (Drawing by Herbert Knöetel, courtesy of The Company of Military Historians.)

son duty around Trois Rivieres, Canada, until returned to Germany, 1783.[52]

COMMANDER: Colonel J.G. von Ehrenkrook

Fusilier Regiment Erbprinz, 1776-1783: **Musketeer Regiment Prinz Frederich,** 1783 (Hesse Cassel)   Arrived at New York, August, 1776, fighting at Fort Washington. Stationed there until sent to Virginia, March, 1781, and interned at Yorktown. Returned to Germany, 1783. Strength: 502 men left New York for Virginia and 454 men were interned at Yorktown. Uniform: Rose facings until 1783, when changed to crimson, white small clothes, white metal caps to 1783 when replaced with cocked hats; officers' lace, silver.

CHIEF: Erbprinz Wilhelm of Hesse, to 1783
Prinz Frederich of Hesse, 1783 to war's end
COMMANDER: Major General J.D. Stirn, to 1779
Major General F. von Hachenburg, 1779-1783
Colonel F. von Cochenhausen, 1783 to war's end

Fusilier Regiment Erbprinz   (see Fusilier Regiment Lieb)

Grenadiere Regiment Erbprinz   (see Hesse Hanau Regiment)

Regiment von Eyb   (see 1st Regiment Anspach-Beyeruth)

Free Corps of Light Infantry (Hesse Hanau)   Raised in Germany, January, 1781, arriving in New York, August, 1781. A poorly disciplined corps, the unit did patrol duty around the city, leaving it and returning to Germany, July, 1783. Disbanded on return. Strength: one lieutenant colonel, one major, one surgeon, one paymaster and his attendant, one provost and one gunsmith, a rifle company of three officers and 157 men and four light infantry companies of the same makeup. Uniform: Green coats with red collars and cuffs and no lapels, half boots, the light company in leather caps while the rest in cocked hats.[53]

COMMANDER: Lieutenant Colonel M. Janecke

4th Battalion Grenadiere von Graff   (see 4th Battalion Grenadiere von Koehler)

Showing the contrasting splendor in which the officers and men of the Fusilier Regiment Erbprinz began the war with how they ended it are the fusilier and officer of 1775, left, and the officer and corporal of 1780, right. (Drawing by Herbert Knöetel, courtesy of The Company of Military Historians.)

Regiment von Hardenberg (Hanover)   Part of the garrison of
Gibraltar during the siege.[54]

The Hesse Hanau Regiment (Hesse Hanau)   Arrived Quebec,
June, 1776, and served in the Burgoyne campaign, being interned at
Saratoga. Strength: 668 men. Uniform: Red facings, yellow small
clothes, white brandenbergs, white grenadier caps of metal.
   CHIEF: The Count of Hesse Hanau (who was also the Erbprinz of
      Brunswick)
   COMMANDER: Colonel W.R. von Gall

Garrison Regiment von Huyn, 1776-1780: **Garrison Regiment von Ben-
ning,** 1780 to war's end (Hesse Cassel)   Arrived at New
York, October, 1776, fighting at Fort Washington. Sent to Newport,
November, 1776, returning to New York and being sent to Charles-
ton, December, 1779. Part of the garrison there, returning to New
York, November, 1782, and Germany, November, 1783. Strength,
August, 1778: 19 officers, 496 other ranks. Uniform: Yellow collar
and cuffs, no lapels, yellow small clothes; officers' lace, silver.
   CHIEF: Colonel J.C. von Huyn, to 1780
      Colonel F. von Benning, 1780 to war's end
   COMMANDER: Colonel J.C. von Huyn, to 1778
      Lieutenant Colonel L.F. Kurtz, 1778-1780
      Colonel F. von Benning, 1780 to war's end

Anspach Jaegers (Anspach-Beyreuth)   Three companies of four
officers and 97 other ranks each, arriving with and attached to the
Hesse Cassel Jaegers. The second company served at New York, in
the 1777 Philadelphia campaign, the 1780 Charleston siege, while
300 men were at the siege of Fort Stanwix, August, 1777. After the
capture of all the other Anspachers at Yorktown, the unit was
redesignated the Field Jaeger Battalion, of six companies, and all
Anspachers were transferred to it, March, 1782. Returned to Germany, August, 1783. Uniform: Green coats faced crimson, white
breeches and green waistcoats.

   1ST COMPANY COMMANDER: Captain C.G. von Cramon, to July,
      1778

Brunswick Jaeger Company

Captain C.G.J. von Waldenfels,
July, 1778 to war's end
2ND COMPANY COMMANDER: Captain C.G.J. von Waldenfels, to
July 1778
Captain F.W. von Roder, July, 1778
to war's end
3RD COMPANY (AND FIELD BATTALION)
COMMANDER: Lieutenant Colonel C.L.R. Baron von Reitzenstein

Brunswick Jaeger Company　　　Arrived at Quebec, September, 1776, serving with Light Infantry Battalion von Barner (which see.) Uniform: Green coat lined green and faced red, yellow buttons, green waistcoats and buff breeches, grey gaiters.[55]
COMMANDER: Captain M.C.L. Schottelius

Jaeger Corps (Hesse Cassel)　　　Arrived at New York in two divisions, August and October, 1776. Elements of this corps served at virtually every major action of the war in America, many men being interned at Yorktown. Returned to Germany, November, 1783. Strength: 500. Uniform: Green coats faced and lined crimson, green small clothes, although white small clothes were worn in summer, brown leggings, officers' lace, gold.[56]
COMMANDER: Colonel C.E.C. von Donop, to 1777
Lieutenant Colonel L.J.A. von Wurmb, 1777 to war's end

Garrison Regiment von Knöblauch　　　(see Garrison Regiment von Wissenbach)

Fusilier Regiment von Knyphausen (Hesse Cassel)　　　Arrived at New York, August, 1776, fighting at Fort Washington and White Plains. Sent to Trenton, N.J., where surprised December, 1776. Survivors returned to New York and placed in Combined Regiment von Loos for 1777 campaign. That unit was split into two units, December, 1777, and thereafter reformed under its old name. Sent to Quebec, September, 1779, however, suffered heavy losses in a storm at sea, returning to New York and not being sent to Quebec

Mounted and foot men of the Hesse Cassel Field Jaeger Corps. (Drawing by Herbert Knöetel, courtesy of The Company of Military Historians.)

again until May, 1780. Returned to New York, October, 1781, and to Germany, 1783. Strength, October, 1778: 466 men. Uniform: Black facings, yellow small clothes, brass caps.

CHIEF: Lieutenant General W. von Knyphausen
COMMANDER: Colonel H. von Borck

4th Battalion Grenadiere von Koehler, to 1777: **4th Battalion Grenadiere von Graff,** 1777-1782: **4th Battalion Grenadiere von Platte,** 1782 to war's end (Hesse Cassel)   Arrived at New York, October, 1776, fighting at Fort Washington, the raid on Amboy, N.J., June, 1777, the attack on Forts Clinton and Montgomery. Returned to Germany, 1783. Sometimes called the Garrison Grenadiere Regiment, as it was composed of the grenadier companies of the four garrison regiments in America. Strength; October, 1778: 336.

COMMANDER: Lieutenant Colonel von Koehler, to 1777
Lieutenant Colonel von Graff, 1777 to 1782
Lieutenant Colonel von Platte, 1782 to war's end

Musketeer Regiment Landgraf   (see Musketeer Regiment von Wutgenau)

2nd Battalion Grenadiere von Lengerke   (see 2nd Battalion Grenadiere von Block)

Lieb Infantry Regiment, to 1783: **Musketeer Regiment Erbprinz,** 1783 to war's end (Hesse Cassel)   Arrived at New York, August, 1776, fighting at Fort Washington and White Plains. Sent to Rhode Island, November, 1776, returning to New York, May, 1777. Sent to Philadelphia, 1777, fighting at Brandywine and Germantown. Returned to New York with the Army, 1778, staying there until returned to Germany, 1783. Strength; October, 1778: 450. Uniform: Bright yellow facings with white brandenbergs, yellow small clothes, red stocks; officers' lace, silver.

CHIEF: Landgraf Friederich II, to 1783
Erbprinz Wilhelm, 1783 to war's end
COMMANDER: Colonel F.W. von Lossberg to 1780
Major General C.E. von Bischhausen, 1780-1782
Major General F.W. von Wurmb, 1782 to war's end

Lieb Infantry Regiment of 1783 (see Musketeer Regiment von Wutgenau)

1st Battalion Grenadiere von Linsingen (Hesse Cassel)   Arrived at New York, August, 1776. Contained two companies of grenadiers of Hessian Guard Regiments, under Captains Webern and Plessen. Sent on the 1777 Philadelphia campaign, fighting at Brandywine, Germantown and Red Bank, N.J. Returned with the Army to New York, 1778, and sent to Charleston, November, 1779. Returned to New York, November, 1782, and to Germany, 1783. Strength, October, 1778: 352. Uniform: Brick red facings with white brandenbergs, yellow small clothes, white grenadier caps (on the Guard grenadiers).

COMMANDER: Lieutenant Colonel O.C.W. von Linsingen

Combined Regiment von Loos (Hesse Cassel)   Made up in January, 1777, of survivors of the Trenton disaster, and sent on the 1777 Philadelphia campaign, fighting at Brandywine. Upon return to New York with the main army, 1778, the battalion was turned into two battalions and then into the old parent organizations.

COMMANDER: Colonel J.A. von Loos

Fusilier Regiment von Lossburg (Alt) (Hesse Cassel)   Arrived at New York, August, 1776, fighting at Fort Washington and White Plains. Assigned to Trenton, N.J., where surprised, December, 1776. Survivors put into Combined Regiment von Loos for 1777 Philadelphia campaign. Upon returning to New York with the Army, 1778, unit split into two battalions, December, 1777, and then into old organization. Sent to Quebec, September, 1779, suffering heavily from losses in a storm at sea. Survivors returned to New York and sent again to Quebec, May, 1780, where they spent the war until returned to Germany, 1783. Strength, October, 1778: 454. Uniform: Orange facings, white small clothes, brass fusilier caps; officers' lace, gold.

CHIEF: Major General H.A. von Lossburg

COMMANDER: Colonel H.A. von Heeringen, to 1778
Colonel J.A. von Loos, 1778-1782
Colonel F. Scheffer, 1782 to war's end

Musketeer Regiment Jung von Lossburg   (see Musketeer Regiment von Mirbach)

3rd Battalion Grenadiere von Lowenstein   (see 3rd Battalion Grenadiere von Minnigerode)

Regiment La Motte (Hanover)   Part of the garrison of Gibraltar during the siege.[57]

3rd Battalion Grenadiere von Minnigerode, to 1779: **3rd Battalion Grenadiere von Lowenstein,** 1779 to war's end (Hesse Cassel)   Arrived at New York, August, 1776, fighting at Fort Washington. Sent on the 1777 Philadelphia campaign, fighting at Brandywine, Germantown and Red Bank, N.J. Returned with the Army to New York, 1778, and sent to Charleston, early 1780. Returned to New York, November, 1782, and then to Germany, 1783. Strength, October, 1778: 347.
> COMMANDER: Lieutenant Colonel von Minnigerode, to October, 1779
> Lieutenant Colonel F.H. von Schuter, October, 1779-1781
> Lieutenant Colonel von Lowenstein, 1781 to war's end

Musketeer Regiment von Mirbach, to 1780: **Musketeer Regiment Jung von Lossburg,** 1780 to war's end (Hesse Cassel)   Arrived at New York, August, 1776. Sent on 1777 Philadelphia campaign, fighting at Brandywine and Red Bank, N.J. Returned to New York, December, 1777, and stationed there until returned to Germany, 1783. Uniform: Red facings trimmed with plain white lace, white small clothes, red stocks; officers' lace, silver.
> CHIEF: Major General W. von Mirbach, to 1780
> Major General W. von Lossburg, 1780 to war's end
> COMMANDER: Colonel J.A. von Loos, to 1777
> Colonel von Block, 1777-1779
> Colonel C.C. von Romrod, 1777 to war's end
> FIELD COMMANDER: Lieutenant Colonel von Schieck, to October, 1777

Lieutenant Colonel H. von Borck, October,
1777 to war's end

4th Battalion Grenadiere von Platte   (see 4th Battalion Grenadiere
von Koehler)

Musketeer Regiment Prinz Carl (Hesse Cassel)   Arrived at New
York, August, 1776, fighting at White Plains. Sent to Newport,
November, 1776, and returned to New York, May, 1777. Sent to
Charleston, December, 1779, and returned to New York, November,
1782, and to Germany, 1783. Uniform: Red facings trimmed with
yellow lace, white small clothes, red stocks; officers' lace, gold.
    CHIEF: Prinz Carl of Hesse
    COMMANDER: Major General M.C. Schmidt, to 1780
                     Major General D.V. von Gosen, 1780 to war's
                     end

Regiment Prinz Friedrich (Brunswick)   Arrived at Quebec, June,
1776. Small detachment in the Burgoyne campaign and interned at
Saratoga, while some 450 men left at Fort Ticonderoga. Spent the
war in Canada until returned, 1783. Strength: 27 officers, 653 other
ranks. Uniform: Yellow facings, yellow buttons, white small
clothes.[58]
    CHIEF: Lieutenant General Prinz Friedrich August of Brunswick
    COMMANDER: Major General E.H. von Stammer
    FIELD COMMANDER: Lieutenant Colonel C.J. Prätorius

Dragoon Regiment Prinz Lüdwig (Brunswick)   Arrived at
Quebec, June, 1776. Served in the Burgoyne campaign, being interned at Saratoga, except a detachment of 150 men lost at Bennington, Vt. Survivors in Canada continued to draw reinforcements
and reached a strength of 282 men by 1779. Returned to Germany
from Canada, 1783. Strength: 20 officers, 316 other ranks. Uniform:
Light blue coats faced and lined in yellow, white aiguillettes, yellow
buttons, cocked hats with white plumes, yellow small clothes, leggings when dismounted.[59]
    CHIEF: Prinz Ludwig Ernst of Brunswick
    COMMANDER: Major General Baron F.A. von Riedesel

Grenadiere Regiment—von Rall, Etc.

FIELD COMMANDER: Lieutenant Colonel F. Baum, to August, 1777
Major J.C. von Meibom, August, 1777 to war's end

Grenadiere Regiment von Rall, to 1776: **Grenadiere Regiment von Wöllwarth,** 1776-1778: **Grenadiere Regiment von Trümbach,** 1778-1780: **Grenadiere Regiment d'Angelelli,** 1780 to war's end (Hesse Cassel)   Arrived at New York, August, 1776, fighting at Fort Washington and White Plains. Surprised at Trenton, N.J., December, 1776, after which survivors were posted to the Combined Battalion von Loos for the 1777 campaign. Upon return to New York, 1778, returned to old designation, after being split into two battalions, December, 1777. Sent to East Florida, November, 1778, and then to the defense of Savannah, where the regiment lost heavily. Sent to Charleston, July, 1780. Returned to New York, November, 1782, and to Germany, 1783. Uniform: Red collar and cuffs, no lapels, yellow small clothes, brass grenadier caps, red stocks; officers' lace, gold.

CHIEF: Colonel J.G. Rall, to December, 1776
Colonel W.F. von Wöllwarth, 1776-1778
Lieutenant General L. von Trümbach, 1778-1782
Lieutenant General le Marquis d'Angelelli, 1782 to war's end

COMMANDER: Colonel J.G. Rall, to December, 1776
Colonel W.F. von Wöllwarth, 1776-1778
Colonel J.C. von Köehler, 1778-1782
Colonel M. Hatzfeld, 1782 to war's end

Regiment von Reden (Hanover)   Part of the garrison of Gibraltar during the siege.[60]

Regiment von Rhetz (Brunswick)   Arrived at Quebec, September, 1776, taking part in operations on Lake Champlain. As a part of the Burgoyne campaign, interned at Saratoga. Survivors merged into Regiment von Ehrenkrook, serving in the Trois Rivieres area of Canada until returned to Germany, 1783. Strength: 27 officers, 653 other ranks. Uniform: White facings, white small clothes; officers' lace, silver.[61]

An ensign with the regimental colour, a private and a field officer in campaign dress of the Regiment von Rhetz. (Drawing by Frederick Ray, courtesy of The Company of Military Historians.)

Musketeer Regiment von Riedesel

        CHIEF: Major General A.W. von Rhetz

        FIELD COMMANDER: Lieutenant Colonel J.G. von Ehrenkrook

                              Major B.B. von Lucke, for Saratoga campaign

Musketeer Regiment von Riedesel (Brunswick)   Arrived at Quebec, June, 1776 and history and strength same as Regiment von Rhetz (which see.) Uniform: Yellow facings, blue and white striped overalls while serving in America, white pompon with yellow center on cocked hats.[62]

        CHIEF: Major General Baron F.A. von Riedesel

        FIELD COMMANDER: Lieutenant Colonel E.L.W. von Speth

Garrison Regiment von Seitz   (see Garrison Regiment von Stein)

Regiment Seybothen   (see 2nd Anspach-Beyereuth Regiment)

Scheither Corps (Hanover)   In 1775 Lieutenant Colonel G.H.A. von Scheither was granted authority to raise a volunteer corps for service in America of 4,000 men. He failed to raise this many men and, giving up recruiting, he left Germany 26 March, 1776, with 250 men who were merged into British regiments upon their arrival in New York.[63]

Musketeer Regiment von Specht (Brunswick)   Arrived Quebec, September, 1776. History and strength the same as Regiment von Rhetz (which see.) Uniform: Red facings, yellow buttons, white small clothes, white pompons with a red center on the cocked hats.[64]

        CHIEF: Colonel J.F. Specht

        COMMANDER: Major C.F. von Ehrenkrook

Garrison Regiment von Stein, to 1778: **Garrison Regiment von Seitz,** 1778-1783: **Garrison Regiment von Porbeck,** 1783 to war's end (Hesse Cassel)   Arrived at New York, October, 1776, fighting at Fort Washington. Sent to Halifax, September, 1778, where the unit spent the war, leaving there for Germany, August, 1783.

A musketeer, Regiment von Riedesel. The standard breeches and long gaiters were abandoned in favor of gaitered trousers during the Burgoyne campaign. (Drawing by Dennis Martin, courtesy of the *Brigade Dispatch*.)

Musketeer Regiment von Türmbach, Etc.

Strength, October, 1778: 78 officers, 439 other ranks. Uniform: Orange collar and cuffs, no lapels, white small clothes; officers' lace, silver.

CHIEF: Lieutenant General J.L.F. von Stein, to 1778
Colonel F.C.E. von Seitz, 1778-1783
Colonel F. von Porbeck, 1783 to war's end
COMMANDER: Lieutenant Colonel von Kitzel

Musketeer Regiment von Türmbach, to 1778: **Musketeer Regiment von Bose,** 1778 to war's end (Hesse Cassel) Arrived at New York, August, 1776, and sent to East Florida, November, 1778, serving at the siege of Savannah. Sent to Charleston, December, 1779, fighting at Stono Ferry, Guilford Court House and Eutaw Springs. With the Army in Virginia and interned at Yorktown. Uniform: White facings with a variety border and buttonholes, white small clothes, red stocks; officers' lace, gold.

CHIEF: Major General L. von Türmbach, to 1778
Major General C. von Bose, 1778 to war's end
COMMANDER: Colonel C.E. von Bischhausen, to 1780
Lieutenant Colonel B.H. von Münchhausen, 1780 to war's end

Grenadiere Regiment von Trumbach   (see Grenadiere Regiment von Rall)

Regiment von Voit   (see 1st Regiment Anspach-Beyeruth)

3rd Waldeck Regiment (Waldeck)   Raised specifically for British service, May, 1776 and arrived in New York, October, 1776, fighting at Fort Washington and the defense of Staten Island. Sent to Pensacola, West Florida, October, 1778, where served until that post fell, May, 1781, then being sent for a month to Havana, Cuba as prisoners, before being paroled to New York. Returned to duty there, July, 1782, until returned to Germany, July, 1783. Strength: 24 officers, 650 infantrymen, two 3 lb. guns and 14 artillerymen. Uniform: Bright yellow facings, white small clothes.[65]

COMMANDER: Lieutenant Colonel J.L.W. von Hanxleden, to January, 1781

Lieutenant Colonel A. von Horn, January, 1781 to war's end

Garrison Regiment von Wissenbach, to 1780: **Garrison Regiment von Knoblauch,** 1780 to war's end (Hesse Cassel)   Arrived at New York, October, 1776, fighting at Fort Washington. Sent to East Florida November, 1778, and to Savannah, December, 1778. Fought at Stono Ferry, S.C., while 80 men were sent to St. Augustine, East Florida. Returned to New York, August, 1782, and to Germany, 1783. Uniform: White facings until lapels removed in 1783, whereafter black collar and cuffs, white small clothes; officers' lace, silver.

    CHIEF: Lieutenant General M.A. von Wissenbach, to 1780
           Major General H. von Knoblauch, 1780 to war's end
    COMMANDER: Colonel A. von Horn, to 1778
           Lieutenant Colonel F. von Porbeck, 1778 to war's end

Grenadiere Regiment von Wöllwarth   (see Grenadiere Regiment von Rall)

Musketeer Regiment von Wutgenau, to 1776: **Musketeer Regiment Landgraf,** 1776-1783: **Lieb Infantry Regiment,** 1783 to war's end (Hesse Cassel)   Arrived at New York, October, 1776, fighting at Fort Washington. Sent to Newport, November, 1776, returning to New York, June, 1779, staying there until returned to Germany, 1783. Strength, August, 1778: 16 officers, 508 other ranks. Uniform: Red collar and cuffs, no lapels, decorated with white brandenbergs with two orange worms, yellow small clothes, red stocks; officers' lace, gold.

    CHIEF: General H.W. von Wutgenau, to 1776
           Landgraf Friedrich II, 1776 to war's end
    COMMANDER: General H.W. von Wutgenau, to 1776
           Colonel H.A. von Heeringen, 1776-1777
           Major General C. von Bose, 1777-1778
           Major General H.J. von Kospoth, 1778 to war's end

One of the units sent to India was the 2nd Battalion/42nd (Royal Highland) Regiment of Foot. Thomas Uschold wears a reconstruction of a regimental pioneer's uniform. He wears a fatigue cap made of an old regimental coat, a leather apron, and carries an axe (on belt).

APPENDIX A

The East India Company's Bombay Army

DURING THE PERIOD 1775-1783 the East India Company maintained its own force in India to protect its factories against rebelling Indians and foreign powers.

The Company had a regiment of cavalry, The Governor-General's Bodyguard, with red coats, blue facings and officers' metal of gold, which was raised in 1773. The Nawab of Oudh raised two regiments of Oudh Cavalry and a 1st Regiment of Light Cavalry in 1776 which entered the company's service in 1777. The uniforms were the same as the Governor-General's Bodyguard, except the officers had silver metal. The Nawab also raised The Kandahar Horse, which he lent to the Company in 1778.

The two regiments of Oudh cavalry were disbanded in 1783.

In addition to the cavalry, the Company depended on its battalions of natives, or sepoys, which were led by British officers. The battalions were also dressed in red coats with blue facings and their officers had silver metal. In 1775 there were four battalions of Bombay Sepoys. The 5th and 6th Battalions of Bombay Sepoys were raised in 1775. A 7th Battalion was raised in 1777 and disbanded in 1785. In 1778 the grenadier companies from the seven battalions were brigaded together in an 8th battalion which was named the Bombay Grenadier Battalion in 1783.

In 1780, as the war spread in India, Bombay Sepoy battalions numbered from nine to 15 were raised. The 8th battalion was amalgamated with the 5th Battalion in 1784, while the 9th Battalion was renamed the 8th in 1784 and disbanded in 1785. All the other battalions raised in 1780 were also disbanded in 1784.

The East India Company's Bombay Army

In addition to the Bombay Sepoys, the Company raised a Marine Battalion in 1775 which also had red coats faced blue and silver metal. In 1778 the Company raised a Portuguese Battalion, from among the many Portuguese in the area, which had green facings on their red coats and silver metal. This battalion was disbanded in 1784.[66]

APPENDIX B

Regiments of Horse

THE WAR OF 1775-1784 was not primarily a mounted man's war. Two regiments, the 16th and 17th Regiments of Light Dragoons were sent to North America for service. The rest of the regiments, except one, were stationed in England, Scotland or Ireland. They included the 1st (King's) Dragoon Guards, 2nd (Queen's Bays) Dragoon Guards, 3rd (Prince of Wales) Dragoon Guards; the 1st, 2nd, 3rd and 4th Irish Horse; and 1st (Royal) Dragoons, 2nd (Royal North British) Dragoons, 3rd (King's Own) Dragoons, 4th (Queen's Own) Dragoons, 5th (Royal Irish) Dragoons, 6th (Inskilling) Dragoons, 7th (Queen's Own) Dragoons, and the 8th (King's Royal Irish) Dragoons.

In 1783 dragoon regiments from the numbers above nine were redesignated light dragoons. These included the 9th, 10th (Prince of Wales), 11th, 12th (Prince of Wales), 13th, 14th, 15th (King's), 16th, 17th, and 18th. In the summer of 1779 the 19th, 20th, 21st, and 22nd (Hoyroyd's) Regiments of Light Dragoons were raised. These were disbanded in 1783.

At the same time, the 23rd (Burgoyne's) Regiment of Light Dragoons was formed and in late 1782, sent to India. It was the first European cavalry unit to serve in that country. It was redesignated the 19th Light Dragoons in 1783.

A group of the defenders of Pensacola are, from left, an officer of the 16th Regiment of Foot, an ensign of the 1st Battalion of Pennsylvania Royalists, a private of the Waldeck Regiment, and a corporal of the Maryland Loyalists. (Drawing by Dennis Martin. Courtesy The Company of Military Historians).

APPENDIX C

Organization in the American Theater

GENERALLY INDIVIDUAL UNITS were assigned together in brigades, or, in the defense of cities, assigned to specific locations. Some of these assignments for specific times are given.

1777 CAMPAIGN

Philadelphia Expedition - Major General Sir William Howe

Brigade - Brigadier General Matthew
    Brigade of Guards
    The Light Infantry
    The Grenadiers
    The Queen's Rangers
1st Brigade - Major General Vaughan (later Major General Grant)
    4th Regiment of Foot
    23rd Regiment of Foot
    28th Regiment of Foot
    49th Regiment of Foot
2nd Brigade - Major General Grant
    5th Regiment of Foot
    10th Regiment of Foot
    27th Regiment of Foot
    40th Regiment of Foot
    55th Regiment of Foot

3rd Brigade - Major General Grey
    15th Regiment of Foot
    17th Regiment of Foot
    42nd Regiment of Foot
    44th Regiment of Foot
4th Brigade - Brigadier General Agnew
    33rd Regiment of Foot
    37th Regiment of Foot
    46th Regiment of Foot
    64th Regiment of Foot
5th Brigade - Brigadier General Leslie
    71st Regiment of Foot (three battalions)
Hessian Brigade - Major General Stirn
    Lieb Infantry Regiment
    Regiment von Donop
    Regiment von Mirbach
    Combined Battalion von Loos
Reserve
    16th Regiment of Light Dragoons
    Ferguson's Rifle Corps
    Hessian Reserve - Colonel Donop
    Hessian and Anspach Jaegers
    Hessian Grenadiers (three battalions)

Rhode Island Garrison - Major General Prescott

22nd Regiment of Foot
43rd Regiment of Foot
54th Regiment of Foot
Regiment von Stirn
Regiment von Ditfurth
Regiment von Huyn
Regiment von Bunow

New York Garrison - Lieutenant General Knyphausen

45th Regiment of Foot
63rd Regiment of Foot
Regiment Erbprinz
Regiment von Trümbach
Regiment Prinz Carl
Regiment von Stein
Regiment von Bloch
Regiment von Wissenbach

Amboy, N.J., Garrison - Colonel Eby

55th Regiment of Foot
An Anspach Regiment
The Waldeck Regiment

Brunswick, N.J., Garrison - Brigadier General Matthew

7th Regiment of Foot
26th Regiment of Foot
35th Regiment of Foot
38th Regiment of Foot

DISPOSITIONS OF OCTOBER, 1778

New York Garrison - 17,452 effective men

	No. Effectives		*No Effectives*
Royal Artillery	955	Loyal American Regiment	259
16th Light Dragoons	939	Volunteers of Ireland	412
17th Light Dragoons	338	Royal American Reformees	91
1st Light Infantry	385	Guides & Pioneers	159
2nd Light Infantry	430	3rd Battalion/Delancy's	
1st Grenadiers	435	Brigade	188
2nd Grenadiers	347	Queen's Rangers	373
Foot Guards	877	Emerich's Chasseurs	135
7th Regiment	337	6 Cavalry Troops	193
17th Regiment	368	Hessian Jaegers	680
23rd Regiment	423	Regiment von Linsing	352
26th Regiment	312	Regiment von Lingercke	365
33rd Regiment	411	Regiment von Minnegerode	347
37th Regiment	378	Regiment von Köehler	336
42nd Regiment	732	Lieb Infantry Regiment	450
44th Regiment	341	Regiment Prinz Carl	498
57th Regiment	464	Regiment von Trumbach	484
63rd Regiment	336	Regiment Erbprinz	467
64th Regiment	420	Regiment von Donop	458
The Garrison Battalion	225	Regiment von Mirbach	462
2nd Battalion/N.J.		Regiment von Lossburg	454
Volunteers	188	Regiment von Knyphausen	466
4th Battalion/N.J.		Hessian Artillery	373
Volunteers	258		

Troop Deployments/Effective Strengths

Expedition For Florida -
Major General Grant - 5,147 Effectives

	No. Effectives		No Effectives
4th Regiment	508	35th Regiment	525
5th Regiment	524	40th Regiment	517
15th Regiment	434	46th Regiment	524
27th Regiment	553	49th Regiment	521
28th Regiment	521	55th Regiment	520

Rhode Island Garrison - 5,740 Effectives

	No. Effectives		No Effectives
Royal Artillery	117	King's American	
17th Dragoons	13	Regiment	419
22nd Regiment	389	Loyal New Englanders	82
38th Regiment	335	Regiment Landgraf	456
43rd Regiment	455	Regiment von Ditfurth	520
54th Regiment	480	Regiment von Huyn	505
2 flank companies	221	Regiment von Bunau	515
Prince of Wales		1st Anspach Regiment	377
American Regt.	337	2nd Anspach Regiment	396
		Hessian Artillery	123

Embarked For Halifax - 646 Effectives

	No. Effectives		No Effectives
King's Orange Rangers	207	Regiment von Seitz	439

Embarked For East Florida - 3,657 Effectives

	No. Effectives		No Effectives
71st Regiment	1,159	3rd Battalion/N.J.	
1st Battalion/Delancy's		Volunteers	379
Brigade	323	New York Volunteers	318
2nd Battalion/Delancy's		Regiment von Wissenbach	436
Brigade	217	Regiment von Rall	471
1st Battalion/N.J.			
Volunteers	354		

Embarked for West Florida -
1,102 Effectives

	No. Effectives		No Effectives
Pennsylvania Loyalists	165	Waldeck Regiment	660
Maryland Loyalists	277		

Dispositions of New York Garrison -
November, 1781
(No. men fit for duty)

New York City

Royal Artillery	390	Musketeer Regiment	
40th Regiment	245	Landgraf	298
Regiment von Linsing	295	Regiment von Knyphausen	265
Regiment von Lengercke	342	Regiment von Bunau	409
Regiment von Loewenstein	311	Hessian Combined	
		Battalion	245

Hampstead

17th Dragoons	286

Jamaica

1st Grenadiers	506	2nd Grenadiers	424

Paulus Hook

22nd Regiment	378	Light Infantry	
		Detachments	115

Kingsbridge

37th Regiment	373	Hesse Hanau Frie Corps	444
Regiment von Lossburg	407		

Flushing

38th Regiment	366	Loyal American Regiment	123
54th Regiment	332		

Troop Deployments/Effective Strengths

North River Shore

42nd Regiment   626

Flagstaff

57th Regiment   352   3rd Battalion/N.J.
                                                          Volunteers   209

Flatlands

British detachments   141

Herricks, Jericho, Westbury

Hessian Jaegers   787

Yellow Hook

Regiment Prinz Carl   484

Guannas

Lieb Infantry Regiment   448

McGowan's

Regiment von Donop   414

Denyces

Hesse Hanau detachments   47   Brunswick recruits   153

Herricks

Anspach recruits   104

Flatbush

1st Battalion/Delancy's
   Brigade   247

Richmond

1st Battalion/New Jersey
   Volunteers   245

Horn's Hook

Guides & Pioneers   89

Fresh Meadows

American Legion   172

Utrecht

King's American Dragoons   140

Brooklyn

Garrison Battalion   (?)

Hallets Cove

Queen's Rangers   (?)

Springfield

British Legion   (?)

Newtown

Pennsylvania Loyalists)   (Total of
Maryland Loyalists)   173 in
Waldeck Regiment)   these
                                        three.)

The back of a coat of the 1st Regiment of Foot Guards, ca. 1780. (Courtesy National Army Museum)

Strength of the Royal Army

THE FIGURES BELOW include all effective officers and other ranks in Regular, Provincial and German units.

	April 1775	March 1776	August 1777	October 1778	July 1779	September 1780	September 1781	March 1782
British Isles	12,700	16,347	18,446	62,422	67,421	78,437	78,061	78,969
Gibraltar	3,064	3,188	3,141	5,031	4,930	5,786	5,560	5,336
East Indies	—	—	—	1,099	1,009	1,245	1,099	1,062
West Indies	1,983	1,937	3,315	1,751	8,119	11,153	10,087	8,756
North America	6,991	14,374	23,694	52,561	47,624	44,554	47,301	47,223
Elsewhere	2,325	9,284	2,274	2,309	2,588	6,077	7,173	10,961
Total	27,063	45,130	57,637	112,239	131,691	147,152	149,282	150,310

Figures are taken from Lord North's return books in the William Clements Library and are missing those for the Irish Establishment for which there seems to be no continuous series of returns.

A cartridge box plate of a type worn by British Regulars and Provincials.

References

PRIMARY MATERIAL

Available Public Records

Public Records Office, War Office papers
Public Archives of Canada, Provincial muster rolls and the Haldirman
Collection
William Clements Library, Sackville Germain papers
American Philosophical Society, Sol Finestone Collection

Newspapers

Pennsylvania Ledger, September, 1777-June, 1778
Pennsylvania Evening Post, December, 1777-June, 1778
Royal Pennsylvania Gazette, April, 1778-June, 1778
Royal (New York) *Gazette*, issues of 1781-1783
Liverpool Citizen, 8 October, 1887
(London) *Morning Herald*, issues of 1783
The Scots Magazine, February, 1778

Books

Andre, Major John, *Journal Of*, Tarrytown, N.Y., 1930
Army Lists, 1775-1783, London
Diary of an unidentified British officer, Finestone Collection
Lamb, Roger, *Original and Authentic Journal of Occurances During the
Late American War*, Dublin, 1804
Mackenzie, Frederick, *Diary*, Cambridge, 1930
Simcoe, John G., *A History of the Operations of the Queen's Rangers*,
N.Y., 1844
Tarleton, Banistre, *A History of the Campaigns of 1780 and 1781 in the
Southern Provinces of North America*, London, 1787
Uhlendorf, Bernard, *Revolution in America: The Confidential Letters
and Journals of the Adjutant General Major Baurmiester*, New Brunswick, 1957

References

SECONDARY MATERIAL

Books

Bass, Robert, *The Green Dragoon*, New York, 1957

Boatner, Mayo Mark, *Encyclopedia of the American Revolution*, New York, 1966

Brooke, R. *Liverpool as it Was in the Last Quarter of the Eighteenth Century*, Liverpool, 1853

Brown, Wallace, *The Good Americans*, New York, 1969

Brown, Wallace, *The King's Friends*, Providence, 1965

Butler, Lewis, *Annals of the King's Royal Rifle Corps*, Vol. 1, London, 1913

Callahan, North, *Flight From The Republic*, Indianapolis, 1967

Curtis, Edward E., *Organization of the British Army in the American Revolution*, London, 1926

Calver and Bolton, *History Written with Pick and Shovel*, New York, 1950

Darling, Anthony, *Red Coat and Brown Bess*, Ottawa, 1968

Eelking, Max von, *The German Allied Troops in the North American War of Independence*, translated by J.G. Rosengarten, Albany, 1893

Fortescue, J.W., *A History of the British Army*, Vol. III, London, 1902

Fyler, Col., *The History of the 50th or (The Queen's Own) Regiment*, London, 1895

Knight, C.R.B., *Historical Records of the Buffs*, Vol. 1, London, 1935

Lawson, C.C.P., *A History of Uniforms of the British Army*, Vols. III, IV, V, London, 1960

Lefferts, Charles, *A History of the Uniforms of the American, British, French and Germans in the War of the American Revolution, 1775-1783*, New York, 1926

Macksey, Piers, *The War for America*, Cambridge, 1965

Metzger, Charles, *Catholics & The American Revolution*, Chicago, 1962

Nelson, William, *The American Tory*, Oxford, 1961

Parklyn, H.G., *Shoulder Belts and Buttons*, Aldershot, 1956

Picton, *Memorials of Liverpool*, Vol. 1, 1873

Quarles, Benjamin, *The Negro in the Revolution*, Chapel Hill, 1961

Report on the American Manuscripts of the Royal United Institution of Great Britain, Vol. III, London, 1901

Sabine, Lorenzo, *The American Loyalists*, Boston, 1847

Smith, Paul, *Loyalists & Redcoats*, Chapel Hill, N.C., 1964

Sparrow, W.J., *Knight of the White Eagle*, Birmingham, 1964

Stark, J.H., *Loyalists of Massachusetts*, Salem, 1910

Stevens, B.F., *The Campaign in Virginia*, 1781, London, 1888

Touzeau, J., *The Rise and Progress of Liverpool from 1551 to 1835*, Vol. II, Liverpool, 1910

Transactions of the Historical Society of Lancashire and Cheshire, Vol. XXXII, Vol. XLVIII

Wickwire, Franklin & Mary, *Cornwallis*, Boston, 1967

Wilcox, William B., *Portrait of a General*, New York, 1964

Magazines

Brigade Dispatch, The, Journal of the Brigade of the American Revolution
Cole, David, "The 23rd Regt. at Bunker Hill," Vol. VIII, No. 2, p. 3
Troiani, D., "Gunner, 4th Battalion, Royal Artillery Regiment, 1776," Vol. IX, No. 3, pp 8-10
Collections of the New Brunswick Historical Society
Raymond, D.W., "Loyalists in Arms," 1901
Raymond, D.W., "Roster of Provincial Officers," 1901
Collections of the Nova Scotia Historical Society
Piers, Harry, "The Fortieth Regiment, raised in Annapolis Royal in 1717; and Five Regiments Subsequently Raised in Nova Scotia," 1927, p. 158
Journal of the Society for Army Historical Research
Cambridge, The Marquess of, "Notes on the Armies of India," Vols. XLVII, XLVIII
Dornfest, W.T., "The Royal Garrison Battalion," Vol. XLVII, No. 189, p. 55
Haarmann, A.W., "82nd Regiment of Foot: Uniform, 1780," Vol. XLVI, No. 188, p. 248
Haarmann, A.W., "Captain William Stewart's Troop of Provincial Light Dragoons, 1779-1782," Vol. XLVI, No. 188, p. 248
Haarmann, A.W., "British Legion Cavalry and Bucks County Light Dragoons; Uniforms, 1780," Vol. XLVII, No. 189, p. 60
Haarmann, A.W., "Jamaician Provincial Corps, 1780-1783," Vol. XLVIII, No. 193, pp 8-13
Haarmann, A.W., "Notes on the Brunswick Troops—In British Service During the American War of Independence, 1776-1783," Vol. XLVIII, No. 195, pp. 140-143
Haarmann, A.W., "The 3rd Waldeck Regiment in British Service, 1776-1783," Vol. XLVIII, No. 195, pp. 182-185
Haarmann, A.W., "Some Notes on American Provincial Uniforms," Vol. XLIX, No. 199, pp. 141-151
Haarmann, A.W., "The Roman Catholic Volunteers, 1777-1778," Vol. XLIX, No. 199, p. 184
Haarmann, A.W., "The Jamaician Volunteer Corps, 1779-1781," Vol. XLIX, No. 200, p. 249
Katcher, P.R.N., "The First Pennsylvania Loyalist Battalion, 1777-1783," Vol. XLVIII, No. 196, p. 250
Parfitt, G.A., "The 91st Foot or Ackland's Loyal Shropshire Regiment, Otherwise Known as the Shropshire Volunteers, 1779-1783," Vol. XLVII, No. 192, pp. 225-232
Kingsman, The, Journal of the King's Regiment
Author not given, "The Royal Liverpool Blues," Vol. II, December, 1930, No. 3, pp. 29-30
Magazine of Pennsylvania History
Connolly, John, "A Narrative of the Transactions, Imprisonment and Sufferings of John Connolly, an American Loyalist and Lieut. Col. in His Majesty's Service," Vols. 12-13 (1888-1889)
Montresor, Captain John, "Diary of," Vol. 6, p. 204 passim

References

Military Collector & Historian

Chapman, F.T. and Elting, J.R., "The Brunswick Regiment of Dragoons, 1776-1783," Vol. XII, p. 17

Chartrand, Rene, "Notes on Bermuda Military Forces, 1687-1815," Vol. XXII, pp. 73-79

Chartrand, Rene, "Uniforms of the Hesse Cassel Troops Sent to America in 1776," Vol. XXIII, pp. 90-91

Copeland, P.F. and Holst, D.W., "The 16th (Queen's) Regiment of Light Dragoons, 1776-1778," Vol. XV, pp. 116-118

Copeland, P.F. and Haarmann, A.W., "The Provisional Chasseur Companies of Hesse-Cassel During the Revolutionary War," Vol. XVIII, pp. 11-13

Haarmann, A.W., "Provincial Uniform Colors," Vol. XIV, p. 60

Haarmann, A.W., "The Hessian Army & The Corps in North America, 1776-1783," Vol. XIV, pp. 70-75

Haarmann, A.W., "British, German and Provincial Uniforms in the Revolution: Some Notes from Rivington's North American List for 1783," Vol. XIV, pp. 113-120

Haarmann, A.W., and Holst, D.W., "The Hesse Hanau Free Corps of Light Infantry, 1781-1783," Vol. XV, pp. 40-42

Haarmann, A.W., and Holst, D.W., "The Friedrich von Germann Drawings of Troops in the American Revolution," Vol. XVI, pp. 1-9

Haarmann, A.W., "The Army of Brunswick and the Corps in North America, 1776-1777," Vol. XVI, pp. 76-78

Haarmann, A.W., "The Anspach-Bayreuth Troops in North America, 1777-1783," Vol. XIX, pp. 48-49

Holst, D.W., "18th Century Accoutrements of the Royal Artillery," Vol. XVIII, pp. 43-47

Knöetel, H. and Todd, F.P., "Hesse Cassel Field Jaeger Corps, 1776-1783," Vol. VII, p. 46

Knöetel, H., and Elting, J.R., "Hessen-Kassel Fusilier Regt. (1780 Musketeer Regt.) Erbprinz," Vol. XII, pp. 42-44

McBarron, H.C. and Todd, F.P., "British 84th Regiment of Foot (Royal Highland Emigrants) 1775-1783," Vol. XI, p. 109

McBarron, H.C. and Smith, R.F., "The Queen's Rangers (1st American Regiment) 1778-1783," Vol. XXIV, pp. 20-21

Manders, E.I., "British 35th Regiment of Foot, 1777-1778," Vol. XVI, pp. 15-16

Manders, E.I., "Light Company, 4th (King's Own) Regiment, 1774-1776," Vol. XVIII, pp. 90-92

Manders, E.I. and Snook, G.A., "42nd Royal Highland Regiment (The Black Watch), 1784," Vol. XIX, p. 116

Ray, F.E. and Elting, J.R., "The King's American Regiment, 1783 (The 4th American Regiment,)" Vol. XIII, pp. 16-18

Ray, F.E. and Elting, J.R., "The Brunswick Infantry Regiment von Rhetz," Vol. XVII, p. 49

William and Mary Quarterly

Smith, P.H., "The American Loyalist—Notes on Their Organization & Numerical Strength," re-print

Footnotes

1 WO 34/111 f. 32
2 Copeland & Holst, "16th Light Dragoons," *MC&H*
3 Troiani, "Royal Artillery Gunner," *Brigade Dispatch*
4 Knight, *Historical Records of the Buffs*
5 Cole, "The 23rd Regt.," *Brigade Dispatch*
6 Fyler, *History of the 50th*
7 "Royal Liverpool Volunteers," *The Kingsman*
8 McBarron & Todd, "British 84th Regiment," *MC&H*
9 Parfitt, "The 91st Foot," *JSAHR*
10 Smith, "Notes on Provincials," *William & Mary Quarterly*
11 Quarles, *The Negro In The American Revolution*
12 Bass, *The Green Dragoon*
13 Bass, ibid
14 *Pennsylvania Ledger*, 21 February 1778; *Pennsylvania Evening Post*, 17 February, 1778
15 Lawson, *Uniforms of the British Army*, Vol. III
16 Bass, op cit
17 Lefferts, *Uniforms...of the American Revolution*
18 Haarmann, "Jamaican Provincial Corps," *JSHAR*
19 *Scots Magazine* and Raymond, *Transactions of the New Brunswick Historical Society*
20 Haarmann, op cit
21 Haarmann, ibid
22 Haarmann, ibid
23 Haarmann, "Jamaican Volunteer Corps," *JSHAR*
24 Bass, op cit
25 Lawson, op cit, Vol. V, p. 89
26 Sparrow, *Knight of the White Eagle*
27 PAC, Haldirman Collection MG21, Vol. B122

Footnotes

28 Lawson, op cit, Vol. III
29 Haarmann, "Jamacian Provincial Corps," op cit
30 Connolly, "The Sufferings of," *Pennsylvania Magazine*
31 Lawson, op cit, Vol. III
32 Mackenzie, *Diary*
33 PAC, M623, DL, Vol. 24, p. 392
34 Piers, *Collections of the Nova Scotia Historical Society*
35 Katcher, "Pennsylvania Loyalists," *JSAHR*
36 Lawson, op cit, Vol. V, p. 90
37 Katcher, op cit
38 Haarmann, "Captain William Stewart's Troop..." *JSAHR*
39 Lawson, op cit, Vol. V, p. 89
40 McBarron & Smith, "The Queen's Rangers," *MC&H*
41 Haarmann, "The Roman Catholic Volunteers," *JSAHR*
42 Haarmann, "Jamacian Volunteer Corps," op cit
43 Piers, op cit
44 Dornfest, "The Royal Garrison Battalion," *JSAHR*
45 Lawson, op cit, Vol. III
46 Haarmann, "Provincial Uniforms," *JSAHR*
47 Eelking, *The German Allied Troops*
48 Haarmann, "Notes on the Brunswick Troops," *JSAHR*
49 Haarmann, ibid
50 Haarmann, ibid
51 Copeland and Haarmann, "The Provisional Chasseur Companies of Hesse-Cassel," *MC&H*
52 Haarmann, "Notes on Brunswick Troops," op cit
53 Haarmann and Holst," The Hesse Hanau Free Corps," *MC&H*
54 Fortescue, *History of the British Army,* Vol. III
55 Haarmann, "Notes on the Brunswick Troops," op cit
56 Knöetel and Elting, "Hessen Cassel Field Jaeger Corps," *MC&H*
57 Fortescue, op cit
58 Haarmann, "Notes on the Brunswick Troops," op cit
59 Haarmann, ibid
60 Fortescue, op cit
61 Haarmann, "Notes on the Brunswick Troops," op cit
62 Haarmann, ibid
63 Uhlendorf, *Revolution in America*
64 Haarmann, "Notes on the Brunswick Troops," op cit
65 Haarmann, "The 3rd Waldeck Regiment," *JSAHR*
66 Cambridge, The Marquess of, "Notes on the Armies of India," *JSAHR*

Index

Index

Index

Index

Index